WALK LIKE A BUDDHA

ALSO BY LODRO RINZLER

The Buddha Walks into a Bar . . .

WALK LIKE A BUDDHA

EVEN IF YOUR BOSS SUCKS, YOUR EX IS TORTURING YOU, AND YOU'RE HUNGOVER AGAIN

Lodro Rinzler

 Shambhala / Boston & London / 2013

Shambhala Publications, Inc.
Horticultural Hall
300 Massachusetts Avenue
Boston, Massachusetts 02115
www.shambhala.com

9 8 7 6 5 4 3 2 1

First Edition

Printed in the United States of America
♾ This edition is printed on acid-free paper that meets the
American National Standards Institute Z39.48 Standard.
♻ This book is printed on 30% postconsumer recycled paper.
For more information please visit www.shambhala.com.

Distributed in the United States by Random House, Inc.,
and in Canada by Random House of Canada Ltd

Library of Congress Cataloging-in-Publication Data

Rinzler, Lodro.
Walk like a Buddha: even if your boss sucks, your ex is torturing you,
and you're hungover again / Lodro Rinzler.—First edition.
pages   cm
ISBN 978-1-61180-093-7 (pbk.)
1. Religious life—Buddhism. I. Title.
BQ5405.R56 2013
294.3′444—dc23
2013011861

For Alex. May we all love half as hard as you did.

CONTENTS

Acknowledgments   ix

Introduction   1

1. WAKE UP LIKE A BUDDHA   7

2. PLAY LIKE A BUDDHA   39

3. GETTING IT ON LIKE A BUDDHA   71

4. CHANGE THE WORLD LIKE A BUDDHA   107

5. WORK LIKE A BUDDHA   145

Appendix 1. Sitting Meditation Instruction   179

Appendix 2. Walking Meditation Instruction   183

Notes   185

Resources   189

ACKNOWLEDGMENTS

2012 was the hardest year of my life. I owe an enormous debt to the people who supported me throughout this period. To David Delcourt, Brett Eggleston, Will Conkling, Miranda Stone, Laura Sinkman, and Marina Klimasiewfski, I owe more than words can describe. To Ethan Nichtern, my oldest friend, thank you for continuing to show up. To Oliver Tassinari, Matt Bonaccorso, Sean Gavin, Eric French, and Dilip Sidhu, thank you for being there for me year in and year out. To my parents and siblings, I have great love and appreciation for you.

This book was written over a period of six weeks in New York City beginning in December 2012. I was without a home during that time, but wonderful people took me in and gave me space to work from. Ericka Philips became more than a partner-in-crime, allowing me to work from her Harlem apartment for the majority of that time, feeding me tea and listening to me lament, all with extreme generosity. Annie Colbert and Tom Krieglstein are terrific friends to have, and allowed me to take over their Lower East Side apartment for a spell. Last but not least, Kelsey Merritt let me monopolize her home in Union Square whenever I wanted and provided excellent music and company during that time.

More than one hundred people wrote in with questions for this book. I would like to thank at least some of those people: Molly Parr, Mia Baxter, Meghan Sultana, Rob Codling,

Jose Rodriguez, Stephanie Elliot, Jason Bequette, Jesee, Ryan Nausieda, JC, Mona, John Globiemski, Michael, Pat Groneman, Cody McGough, Jess Auerbach, Lynne, and Jessica Carsten.

I am lucky enough to work with the best people in the publishing business, including Jonathan Green, Sara Bercholz, Julie Saidenberg, Steven Pomije, Daniel Urban-Brown, and Stephanie Tade. My editor, Dave O'Neal, is the best thing since sliced bread. Thank you all for your incredible care in bringing this book to life.

One final thank-you must be directed to all of the teachers and mentors who have guided me on the Buddhist path. My appreciation is fathomless. In particular, I owe credit for whatever small amount of wisdom that has been laid to paper here to my root teacher, Sakyong Mipham Rinpoche.

WALK LIKE A BUDDHA

INTRODUCTION

Straight off the bat, I should mention that I'm sort of a mess and also okay. Sometimes I'm sad or angry, and yet I'm also confident that at my core I am a buddha. I'm not alone in that belief. A core tenet of Buddhism is that we are all already awake. At the same time, we don't normally act from that perspective; we often act from our confusion instead. So in a sense, we're all sort of a mess (acting confused) but also okay (inherently awake).

If you're reading this you may not necessarily be a Buddhist, which is great. Or maybe you are but realize you're not the perfect meditator (who is?). Either way, I am guessing that you have some inkling that while there are major upsets in life and sometimes you may act inappropriately, you aren't such a bad guy or gal. That you might even buy in to this idea that at your core you're innately kind, wise, and worthy.

At one point the Zen master Suzuki Roshi turned to his students and said, "All of you are perfect just as you are . . . and you could use a little improvement."[1] That seems to be the case with all of us. We are already perfect. We are already Buddha. And we need to stop acting from the basis of our own confusion (read: acting like a jerk). The slight shift toward improvement that Suzuki Roshi mentions is based on developing unconditional faith in your own ability to be awake. It is recognizing that the mess aspect of who you are is transitory, while the awake quality is always available and present.

Several years ago I hatched a plan to write a book about Buddhism and this particular topic for people in my generation, Generation Y. I was in Japan for a few months and jotted down some initial thoughts that, frankly, didn't go anywhere. So I meditated a lot and waited for a better time to do that work.

When I returned to New York City, I went out to eat with my friend Ethan Nichtern. He encouraged me to start my writing by doing regular blog posts. Together over brunch we hatched an idea for a weekly Buddhist advice column known as *What Would Sid Do?* Sid, in this case, was short for Siddhartha. Abbreviating the name was not meant as any disrespect for the man who went on to become the Buddha, but you know, I thought that maybe his close friends might have called him just Sid while growing up. Do you really think they didn't have nicknames twenty-six hundred years ago?

The idea behind the abbreviation, and the column as a whole, is that before Siddhartha Gautama attained enlightenment, he was a confused twenty- and thirty-something looking to learn how to live a spiritual life. In the column, we looked at what it might be like if a fictional Siddhartha were on his spiritual journey today. How would he combine Buddhism and dating? How would he handle stress in the workplace? *What Would Sid Do?* was devoted to taking an honest look at what we as meditators face in the modern world.

Upon its inception, people began writing in with questions about how they could apply Buddhist principles to their everyday life. No subject was considered taboo. In fact, the first topic that came up on the column was about what to do when you wake up next to a stranger after a night of sex. I recommended some traditional teachings around communication and some advice around taking your bedmate out to brunch. As you may suspect, I really like brunch. After that, topics came in from all over the world, ranging from developing a meditation practice to going out on the town to romantic entanglements to social action to work. While only the littlest bit of the previously published work is in these pages, all of those topics are covered in-depth within this volume.

As I began to work on my first book, *The Buddha Walks into a Bar*, the column went on the back burner. When that book came out, something unique happened. It sparked a dialogue around what it means to practice Buddhism and meditation in today's world. In both the column and the book, people felt engaged enough to write to me and continue to ask questions, or spark debate, around how we can apply Buddhist principles to our life. As I traveled to approximately thirty cities in 2012 alone, doing book events, this discussion grew and grew.

When I did workshops, people would write down questions at the end of our time together. We would contemplate them as a group, and I would shut up and let the participants bring their own wisdom to bear on how qualities cultivated through meditation, such as gentleness, or how traditional teachings like the six *paramitas* (more about the *paramitas* later), could address the hard issues that were coming up in people's lives.

All of this said, to circle back to my original "I'm a mess and I'm also okay" statement, the *What Would Sid Do?* column, the first book, and this thing you are holding in your hand now: it's not about me and my advice. It's about me getting out of my own way and trying to articulate what little I know about the Buddhist dharma, or teachings, and how I have worked with these issues over the years.

Let's face it—I'm not the superlearned monk at your local monastery. I'm a guy who was raised Buddhist, who has spent more hours on his butt meditating than he might normally admit, but who got serious about all of this stuff at an age when he was also starting to do things like drink with friends and date and, eventually, work. Having brought my meditation practice to these aspects of my life as soon as they started, I have gotten comfortable offering my experience with the caveat that I am not some holy teacher but someone who is in a unique position to open the discussion around making Buddhism and meditation applicable to society and to daily life today.

I became a regular meditation practitioner relatively early on. While I started meditation at the age of six, I didn't get serious about it until my teenage years. When I was seventeen, my parents turned to me and said, "You know what would make for a great college essay? Spending your summer at this monastery." They thrust a pamphlet into my hand for Gampo Abbey, the Shambhala monastic facility in rural Nova Scotia. I shrugged and acquiesced. Off to the monastery I went.

Fast-forward to the following fall—and my parents were right: shaving my head and taking temporary ordination as a monk did make for a great essay. The unfortunate thing for them is that they had created a monster. They saw this activity as a good thing for me to do with a summer, but it shaped my experience such that all I wanted to do in my four years at college was meditate, study the dharma, and meditate some more. I started a meditation group at Wesleyan University, which then became Buddhist House, a communal living and meditation space on campus. My first job out of college was running a meditation center in Boston. It's only progressed from there.

Early on in my freshman year of college, people would approach me at parties and say, "Aren't you a Buddhist? How come you're drinking alcohol?" Good question, right? I would talk about how monastics take precepts about not ingesting intoxicants and how I wasn't a monk, so it was okay. Yet I would walk away feeling that that wasn't the clearest response for me personally. I felt as if I were justifying binge drinking with a flimsy excuse. So I contemplated my drinking habits, on and off the meditation cushion, and ultimately came to my personal middle way on the issue: I could imbibe, but if I felt that I was no longer being mindful, or present, with what was going on, then I should stop.

It took me years to find that balance of being able to drink without losing my shit. There were times when I would be sober for weeks or months at a time. Other times I overindulged and lived a hungover existence. I seem to have struck a balance at this point, but I realize I may still relapse and have to start fresh in the future. Remember: I'm a mess and also okay.

While I was in college, I found myself in many conversations with my peers around basic Buddhist ideas and how they came to bear on my life. This dialogue allowed me to test the mettle of the Buddha's teachings and see if and how they were relevant to my existence. I am grateful to have started this dialogue early on, so that my meditation practice was always something to be lived as opposed to something that I had to do on a meditation cushion.

At the same time, if there is a mistake to be made on the spiritual path, I've made it. Often I've learned from it. I have taken to heart the advice of the Tibetan Buddhist teacher Chögyam Trungpa Rinpoche when he said, "Live your life as an experiment."[2] Each experiment with drugs or romantic entanglement or fuckup at work has led me toward an opportunity to bring my meditation practice off the cushion and into the rest of my life.

For that, and for the incredible teachers who have pointed the way for me, I am thankful. When I was nineteen years old I became a Vajrayana student of Sakyong Mipham Rinpoche. I have had the opportunity to study in-depth with him and other brilliant, selfless beings. These experiences have shaped me in ways I cannot truly comprehend or express. Their teachings, matched with my proclivity for both messing up and meditating, have spiraled into the creation of this book.

The questions in the book come from people who have e-mailed me, asked them in my travels, or casually offered them up over drinks. They are real questions from real people. My answers to the questions are based on my meditation practice, study, and experience, but I don't believe that they are "right." I don't think universal "right answers" exist to these questions. The questions can be explored, but the right answer is the one that is your own.

As you go through each question, I encourage you to think

about how you might use Buddhist ideas to effect a positive change in response to the scenario at hand. I have some ideas, and I know you do too. So let's see if we can shed our fixed point of view and explore these issues wholeheartedly. I'll do my best, but as you know, I'm no saint.

I have never professed to be a master of anything. I'm just a guy. But then again, so was Siddhartha. He went on a spiritual journey, made some mistakes along the way, and ultimately became enlightened. You and me, we can do that same thing. Through the practice of meditation, and the cultivation of mindfulness and compassion, we can follow in his footsteps. We can walk like a buddha.

When you are done with this book, please write me and let me know what you think. The dialogue is just beginning.

Lodro Rinzler
East Harlem, New York
December 7, 2012

1 / WAKE UP LIKE A BUDDHA

Meditation is awesome. At its core, it is an exercise anyone can practice that allows us to become more familiar with our own mind and heart. If the Buddha did it and woke up, we can too.

The foundation of this chapter is an exploration of meditation but also of the ins and outs of basic Buddhist philosophy. There are some subtle aspects of traditional Buddhism that people have asked me about with a "you don't really believe this, do you" mentality. There are also basic "how can I get my meditation practice going" questions. We will explore the benefits of meditation on how we live our day-to-day lives. Afterward we will move on to how meditation can be applied to going out on the town, romantic situations, social action, and our work.

What's the Point?

Why meditate? I mean, I hear it's supposed to reduce stress, but it sounds like a lot of work.

The basic meditation practice introduced in the first appendix of this book is known as *shamatha*, or calm-abiding meditation. If you haven't given it a try, I recommend checking out the instructions in the back of the book and using that practice as a complement to reading this volume. As the person asking the question suggests, meditation is a way to bring a sense of calm into a small portion of your life, the time you spend meditating, but it also naturally filters into all of your waking moments over time.

In some sense, meditation is just a practical tool for learning to see your own mind and work with your emotional states. You tune in to the present moment, what is going on this second, and learn to relate to it. You are not relating to it in your habitual way of thinking about what you would like to see happen or how things used to be. You are training in seeing reality as it is right now.

What is going on right now can be stressful. What is going on right now might also be joyful. But it is always real. It is always the reality of the situation. So in that sense, meditation is not going to be a cure-all for stress but is very much going to help you address what your reality is on a moment-by-moment basis.

When you engage in *shamatha* meditation, you focus your concentration on the physical sensation of both your out-breath and your in-breath. The breath is a constant reminder of what is going on in this very moment. It is not a time to think about the past or what you will be doing later. The breath is always now.

Recently I attended a holiday fund-raiser for a homeless aid organization I work with known as the Reciprocity Foundation. My friend Taz, who led the event, offered a short meditation session to get it going. While I don't think Taz would consider herself a "hardcore" Buddhist, she clearly knew the most important things to emphasize. "What happened in the past has already happened," she said. "There is nothing you can do about that. What will happen is in the future. Let's take a moment just to be with what is going on now. Let's leave all of that behind and just be in this room."

I enjoyed that approach because, while it was not formal *shamatha* instruction, it was a clear articulation of the purpose of meditation. The purpose of this practice is not about finding less stress in the past or the future but about letting those notions go and just existing, both while meditating and while out in the world. The purpose of meditation practice is to blur the lines between meditation and postmeditation practice, so that we live all of our waking hours being present to whatever the world presents to us.

In a larger sense, meditation is a way to see through our ignorance and awaken the seed of enlightenment, known as buddha nature or basic goodness. When we look to the example of the Buddha, we see a normal man who left the temptations of his day in order to focus on taming his wild mind. He engaged in the exact practice we can engage in today, *shamatha*. He worked diligently to get to know himself, to see his own layers of confusion, and discovered that underneath it all he was basically good.

I have found that this is a pretty radical notion for anyone who was raised with a strong Christian background. Within that religious tradition there is an emphasis on original sin, which dictates that we are basically not good at all but must work for our salvation. Within the Buddhist tradition we are saying the opposite: actually you are basically good. You are basically wise. You are basically kind. You just need to discover that truth and develop confidence in it.

Sometimes (often) you get confused and don't act from the view of basic goodness, but that perspective of wakefulness is always available to you. In fact, the view of basic goodness isn't even a Buddhist thing. Buddhists don't own it. My root teacher, Sakyong Mipham Rinpoche, has said, "Basic goodness is not confined to any one tradition. It is the essence of everyone and everything."[1] We all possess this seed for awakening.

At any moment we can tap in to our basic goodness. When we rest in this very moment, we follow in the Buddha's footsteps and see past our fixed expectations, our lingering judgments, and our emotional upsets. We see straight to our core, our buddha nature. If we can train ourselves to connect with that fundamental aspect of our being and act from that perspective, as opposed to from our confused mentality, then we will be able to live a rich and full life. We will be awake, which is essentially what we are talking about when we discuss the Buddhist notion of attaining nirvana.

I should say, though, that meditation is indeed hard work. I won't deny that. When you sit down to practice meditation, you may experience more of your own downpour of thoughts than an unceasing experience of goodness. As a result of that difficulty, for beginners it can be a struggle to maintain a regular meditation practice of, say, ten to twenty minutes a day.

The Tibetan Buddhist teacher Chögyam Trungpa Rinpoche once pointed out, "If you put one hundred percent of your heart into facing yourself, then you connect with this unconditional goodness. Whereas, if you only put fifty percent into the situation, you are trying to bargain with the situation, and nothing very much will happen."[2] So while it is hard work, we should put 100 percent of our energy into looking at our basic state so that we can have an experience of our goodness rather than an intellectual understanding of it.

Why is meditation hard work? Well, there are three primary obstacles that seem to get in our way as we engage this tool for facing ourselves:

1. Laziness

Sometimes you wake up early with the intention to meditate, but your bed is just really cozy and it would be a lot easier to get in twenty more minutes of sleep. That is regular old laziness. We have all been there for some task we just don't want to exert ourselves for. When you sit down to meditate, sometimes it can be a joy and you are able to stay with your breath. Often it is a pain, and you may have trouble coming back to your breath, or difficult emotions may arise, or you may just find yourself lost in fantasy for most of your meditation period. This is all very normal and happens to everyone. It's not unusual for you to feel some aversion to this work and for laziness to manifest as a result.

I have a theory that if you walked into a room full of meditators and asked them to raise their hands if they experienced this form of obstacle, every hand in the room would go up. If you followed up with the question, "Who here thinks that makes them the world's worst meditator?" many hands would go up again. The important thing to remember when addressing laziness is not to be so hard on yourself. Everyone can't bear the title World's Worst Meditator. There can be only one, and I'm relatively confident it's not you. If you find yourself struggling, just remember to take it easy on yourself, drop judgment, and motivate yourself to your meditation seat.

2. Speedy-Busyness

As a New Yorker, I identify with this big obstacle a lot: speedy-busyness. In New York everyone thinks he or she is the busiest person in the world. There is always something going on in this city. You could easily fill up every moment of every day with activity. Even if you do not live in a big city, you can fill up all of your time by seeing friends, catching up on news, working late, or doing basic tasks like grocery shopping or laundry. It's easy to be speedy and busy. It seems that the older you get, the busier you are with work responsibilities, romantic commitments, family, and more.

The obstacle of speedy-busyness often manifests as thinking you actually don't have time for meditation. For example, you get up in the morning and think you have time to meditate, but actually, you realize, you have to send a few e-mails before work. Then you rush to work and have a hectic day but commit to meditating when you get home. Right as you are about to clock out, your coworker invites you out for a drink. One drink won't hurt you, you think, so you go get one drink. That drink turns into two, but then you drag yourself home convinced you will meditate when you sober up. You make yourself some tea, and you know you will meditate just as soon as you call your mom. You haven't talked to her in way too long, and you owe her that phone call. After you get off the phone with your mom, you have a bit of time to meditate, but you haven't showered all day and you smell, so you ought to do that. You get out of the shower and look at the time, and it has gotten very late and you're exhausted and you think, "Well, I guess I'll just meditate in the morning." You get up the next morning and do that all over again. That is speedy-busyness. It is the idea that everything else is superimportant and can't wait, except for your meditation practice.

Speedy-busyness is one of the reasons I recommend that people have a set time that they meditate. If you say, "I meditate at 8:00 A.M. every day, Monday to Friday," then you will build out your schedule to include that commitment. It will not keep being shoved to the back burner. So I recommend having a consistent time that you meditate and making that a priority.

3. Disheartenment

The third obstacle commonly associated with getting a meditation practice going is disheartenment. Because it is hard work to get to and stay on the meditation seat, and because we are so trained in instant gratification in today's world, meditation is often taken up and discarded in quick time. We want to see an immediate fix when we pick up a meditation practice.

We are used to quick fixes. If your computer breaks down, you take it to someone who returns it to you within hours, all repaired. If you need books for school, you can order them and have them shipped to your home the next day. This year a significant percentage of people bought luxury automobiles . . . over their mobile phones. The vehicles were custom-made according to instructions transmitted by mobile devices and delivered to customers' doors shortly thereafter. We have become accustomed to seeing quick results following minimal effort.

Meditation is such a gradual path that you don't get to see quick results. It is not something you can try once a month and hope you will magically get "good" at it. First off, there is nothing to get good at. You are just being with your own mind. That's it. So any time you spend with your own mind is good time. Second, it takes not hours or days but weeks and months to see how meditation gradually changes you. These changes are so subtle it is hard to think of meditation as anything other than a gradual path of transformation.

The key antidote to all of these obstacles is having a strong motivation to practice. So, to answer the original question, "Why meditate?" I have to say it's a very personal thing. For me, I find that over the years meditation has made me kinder, or at least less of a jerk. I find that it has made me more present, not just with my breath while meditating, but with conversations with friends and family, with the difficult moments in my life, when I'm kissing someone and enjoying that person's company. It has given me the ability to enjoy my life and feel content within the present moment, regardless of whether what I am experiencing is conventionally good or bad, fun or painful.

Each of us has to come up with our own motivation to meditate. At first it might be something like "I don't want to be so stressed out" or "I want to learn to be comfortable with the strong emotions I am feeling." Those are both great. Over time you may find that your motivation shifts. At first you were in it to better yourself, but gradually your heart has opened and you see that meditation is having a positive effect on your life. Your motivation might transition into "I want to learn more about myself so I can be more present with others" or "I want to be able to be of benefit to the world, and in order to do that, I want to experience my basic goodness."

The bottom line is that you have to meditate for a reason that feels right to you and then give yourself the time to let your meditation practice catch up with that motivation. Because it is so gradual a path, you need to be patient and put in the hours to let it have an effect on you. When you do that, you can reflect back and say, "I guess this meditation stuff is working." It may take weeks, months, or even years, but if you can look back and say, "This is changing me for the better," then you will be motivated to continue doing it for a long time to come.

LEARNING TO BE CONTENT

Is there a relationship between happiness and meditation?

Yes. The beauty of meditation practice is that we can learn to be more present with our world. It is a simple practice, but that also means that it is very workable. As I mentioned before, you might see positive results in your meditation practice after a period of time. If you do end up kinder, more compassionate, or more present in your day-to-day life, then that strikes me as a form of happiness.

At first you may think that meditation is like a pill that you can take. You might think that if you sit in meditation for a certain amount of time every day, that is the rough equivalent of taking a happy pill. That time on the cushion just ought to translate into less stress and more happiness. In that case, you are looking for an easy fix. The difference between pill popping and meditation is that the latter has a tendency to seep into your bones. You are not just prescribing a remedy for your temporary suffering but beginning to look at your suffering overall.

That means that you may not see a connection between meditation and happiness at first. In the beginning, you see a connection between meditation and your own chaotic, confused mind. You might even think that meditation has made you crazier than ever before. Yet gradually, a natural progression occurs with your meditation practice, where it moves from something that you do on the cushion, which may or may not bring you joy depending on what your mind is like that day, to something that is an essential part of a life based on contentment.

This transition is due to the simple skill that you develop:

mindfulness. Mindfulness is known in the Tibetan language as *trenpa,* which bears the longer translation "the ability to hold your attention to something." This something can be your breath, as in *shamatha* meditation, or a statue or burning incense, but it can also be more visceral aspects of your daily life.

For example, you can engage in a simple practice of mindfulness by putting an M&M in your mouth. Don't bite down on it, don't swallow it. Just let it dissolve in your mouth. Pay attention to the changing of tastes as the shell wears away. Notice the flavor of the coloring and of the chocolate. When you notice yourself starting to daydream or your mind beginning to make lists of all of the things you ought to be doing, bring your attention back to the sensation of the M&M dissolving.

The more we train ourselves—both in formal *shamatha* meditation and in other aspects of our life—to hold our attention to what is going on in this moment, the more we begin to appreciate the details of our life. We are mentally slowing down enough to realize the magic of every moment. That may mean raising your gaze and taking in the architecture around you as you go for a run. Or it could be spending time with your young niece and fully being there for her as she tries to articulate whatever is in her mind. Or it may be truly listening to someone who is trying to deliver bad news.

In each of these scenarios, if you are able to be fully present, fully mindful with what is going on, you may find that you experience happiness. The Zen master Seung Sahn told many stories about the Buddha during his teachings. He pointed out that the Buddha said, "If you keep a clear mind moment-to-moment, then you will get happiness everywhere."[3] Happiness, in this context, is just appreciating the world as it is without labeling it as good or bad. The view of basic goodness is that this moment is already sacred and wonderful as long as we can tune in to its innate beauty. If we can have faith that we possess basic goodness and everyone we encounter does as well, then any moment has the potential to be a sacred one.

I want to be clear that this basic level of happiness is a great goal for someone interested in meditation. If you want to get into saying that you're a Buddhist, though, everyday contentment is not really the endgame. The endgame is attaining enlightenment, or nirvana. The Tibetan Buddhist teacher Dzongsar Khyentse Rinpoche has said, "It was not Siddhartha's aim to be happy. His path does not ultimately lead to happiness. Instead it is a direct route to freedom from suffering, freedom from delusion and confusion. Thus nirvana is neither happiness nor unhappiness—it goes beyond all such dualistic concepts. Nirvana is peace."[4]

So while we may start out thinking that we are just in this for less stress or because this idea of being content in the present moment sounds good, the ultimate goal for a Buddhist is actually peace. It is seeing through our suffering and delusion and realizing that we are already a buddha. We are already basically good. That is our innate state. The more we can develop confidence in that reality, the less we will be trapped by our own confusion. Freedom from confusion is nirvana. That sounds pretty good to me.

A CULTURE OF NONDISTRACTION

How do you stay present in an era of constant distraction?

After attaining enlightenment, the Buddha is said to have gotten up, picked up his begging bowl, walked to the nearby stream, and thrown it in. It was a moment of declaration that he had renounced worldly possessions, but I can't help thinking that he must have had a hard time eating after that. Anyway, the Buddha's bowl did something unexpected. In that moment it literally moved against the stream, floating opposite to the current.

I imagine the Buddha took the hint. He knew that everything he would then share about becoming awake to your mind and heart would literally be against the stream of societal norms. He was not wrong about that. The idea of developing mindfulness, the ability to be fully present in the midst of our speedy, chaotic world, is often perceived as far-fetched.

Think about the number of distractions that have been invented even in the last one hundred years. We have television to watch, e-mails to answer, cats to giggle at on YouTube. If anything, it seems that every year leads to an exponential increase in the opportunities to get distracted. It is rare to see new developments in society that encourage you to stay one-pointedly focused on anything. At the time of this writing, AT&T is running a commercial about a new phone. Their tagline is "Doing two things at once is better." In today's culture, multitasking is the new black.

Sakyong Mipham Rinpoche once addressed this issue, noting that we do not do anything one hundred percent anymore. He said, "This quality of speed gives life a superficial feeling; we never experience anything fully."[5] No one strives to live a superficial life. That is not the goal for most people. Through the practice of meditation we can actually learn to experience our lives to the fullest. We can live a profound life, just through learning how not to be distracted.

One of the many Tibetan words for meditation is *samadhi.* Chögyam Trungpa Rinpoche once said, "According to the Buddha's philosophy, there is no verb 'to meditate.' There is just a noun, 'meditation.' There's no meditating. You don't meditate, but you be in a state of meditation. . . . 'Meditation' is a noun that denotes that you are being in a state of meditation *already.*"

Samadhi in this context means that you are one-pointedly there, with whatever is going on in the moment. While a dictionary definition would be "union," the meditation and yoga teacher Michael Stone has translated *samadhi* as "intimacy." It is true intimacy with the present. It is anti-multitasking. One way to think about meditation is that it is the tool that enables you to bring yourself, fully, to one thing. That one thing can be the breath. You can wholeheartedly give yourself over to the simple act of breathing. Or it can be a work assignment. You can one-pointedly focus on that. Or it could be making love. You can bring your whole self to that act. Seung Sahn once gave this instruction: "When you eat, only eating mind; when you drive, only driving mind; when sightseeing, then only sightseeing mind."[6] Whatever you are doing, only do that, and do it fully.

The way to develop this one-pointed concentration is (surprise, surprise) meditation practice. It is a training method in cutting through habitual acts such as multitasking. It is a method to inspire us to be with what is without wishing something more were going on. The more we go against the societal norm of getting distracted, the more we are able just to be. The more we are able just to be, the more we will live a fulfilling life and can be of benefit to others. Imagine what society would look like if more people took on the simple task of cutting through speed and being open to their world as it is. Imagine a culture of nondistraction. That is a world that I want to live in.

MAKING MOVES

I get that meditation is a way to be present. But if you're always present, how can you plan for the future?

I wish we *were* always present. That would be a great problem to have, right alongside your wallet's being too small to hold all of your fifties and your diamond shoes' being too tight. The main issue in our society seems to be the opposite—we're always reliving some event that has already occurred or we are making a zillion plans for the future. We spend so little time actually being fully with whatever is going on in this moment that while I've gotten this question pretty frequently, it always strikes me as more theoretical than experiential.

More often than not, we're constantly planning for the future, and that does not bring us a true sense of happiness. There is an age-old Yiddish saying that seems applicable here: "If you want to make God laugh, tell him your plans." We spend so much of our time thinking through exactly what we want to see happen in the future. When we get to that point in time and everything is not exactly as we imagined it, we end up disappointed. This is the nature of life: the more fixed expectations we carry, the more we are likely to be let down.

For example, you plan a tropical vacation and make a long list of everything you want to do while there: you are going to go snorkeling and dancing and go to this certain island for a day trip. The more plans you make, the less likely that you will fit everything in. Instead of relaxing on your vacation, you are running around with a checklist of things you need to accomplish in order to be happy. That level of activity makes it sound as if you were still at work instead of on some tropical beach. Perhaps instead you might find true contentment in just sticking your toes in the sand and feeling its warmth or looking out at the ocean and relaxing with the calm nature of the waves. In other words, you will likely find more contentment in appreciating things as they are.

To come back to the question, it would be awesome if one were always living in the present moment. If your meditation practice has matured to the point that you are always in the right now, then it is not as if you wouldn't be capable of living a full and rich life. It would only be fuller and richer.

When you slow down enough to appreciate what is going on in this moment, you are following in the footsteps of the Buddha. You are seeing reality as it is as opposed to what you hope it will be or what it once was. You clearly perceive this moment without getting hung up on your particular point of view. Chögyam Trungpa Rinpoche once said, "I am a very ambitious person myself, extremely, dangerously so! However, I relate with *now*."[7] In other words, you can have ambition, and ideas for the future, but they must be rooted in the reality of now.

When you are in tune with the reality of now, it is easy to tell what you ought to do next. The future will come. We know that much. Because everything changes moment by moment, we don't have to worry that the future will not run up to meet us. It is coming. What we can do is clearly perceive what is going on now so as best to meet it.

The more we train through meditation in being attuned to the present, the more we will be prepared to act skillfully in this and every moment of our life going forward. If you are traveling a great deal and working seventy-hour weeks, that takes a toll on your body. It is easy to ignore that, though, and continue to work, sleep when you can, and be swept up in whatever is next on the horizon.

Alternatively, if you are practicing meditation and at least slowing down mentally, then you will see what you are doing to yourself. You will not ignore the signs of fatigue. You will say to yourself, "Uh-oh. I see that I am about to get sick. I'm going to take a break." In that moment you act in the most skillful way possible: you take a day or two off and recharge your body. You might sleep in, exercise, or spend time lounging at home. It is because you were present that you could see that you needed something other than what you were currently doing in order to take care of yourself.

When you are open to what is going on in this very moment, you can discern how best to act. You will be in tune with your own awake nature, and you can let that serve as a moral compass for what you ought to do, be it rest up, go out, change careers, anything. Meditation gives us the ability to see what needs to happen, and then we can act. It is not a robotic state where we can process only what is right in front of us. It gives us a panoramic view of the reality of our situation so that we know how best to direct our energy and take care of ourselves and others long-term. That is the best kind of planning for the future: being open to what is truly going on right now and acting accordingly.

MANTRA AND OTHER MEDITATION PRACTICES

Recently I went to a meditation center, and it seems that they do all sorts of different techniques, such as reciting mantras and doing prostrations. I've meditated on the breath for the last several months. Should I move on to do these other techniques?

Meditation practice can feel boring. There. I said it. At one point during a public talk, Sakyong Mipham Rinpoche acknowledged this notion when he said, "You know, when you meditate, you're only spending time with yourself. So if you are feeling bored, it's not meditation practice that's boring. It's you." Which I am pretty sure is the case, for me at least.

A few years ago I was leading a meditation retreat. The participants weren't brand-new; they had done an introductory weekend before this one. At one point a woman raised her hand and asked, "Is this it? This being with the breath thing? Isn't there something more we can do?" I could certainly have talked about contemplation practice or Vajrayana practices that she could learn down the road, including hand gestures and vast visualization, but my initial response was, "Yes. This is it."

I came down on that woman so heavily because *shamatha* practice is really the best staple you can add to your daily schedule of activities. Just like brushing your teeth, you may enjoy it or you may feel restless while doing it, but it is always good for you. You wouldn't look for something "better" to do with your time instead of brushing your teeth; you know it's one of the things to do to take care of your body. The same can be said for *shamatha* and taking care of your mind.

When I became a Vajrayana student of Sakyong Mipham Rinpoche, he instructed me in a practice known as *ngondro*. *Ngon* can be translated from the Tibetan as "before" and *dro* is "you go." It consists of four preliminary practices you can engage in before you go on to other, advanced Vajrayana teachings. The *ngondro* consists of prostrations, mantra recitation, creation of symbolic mandalas, and a visualization practice involving receiving the blessings of your teacher. At the time, the Sakyong asked each of us students to do each of these practices 108,000 times, except for the last practice, which we were to do 1,080,000 times. Then he told us to complete these practices within the span of three years.

I was eager and threw myself into this work. I felt like a very "good" student as I rapidly progressed along through these practices. I completed the recitations for most of the *ngondro* and went back to the Sakyong two years later to receive more teachings. At that time he instructed the group of Vajrayana students I was a part of to do a different *ngondro* and to measure our progress in it by time spent on each individual practice. So I had to start from scratch after all of my hard work!

I wasn't deterred, though, and completed both of those *ngondro*s over the next year. I went on to receive the empowerments for the visualization practices within two different facets of Shambhala Buddhism and engaged those practices wholeheartedly as well. Somewhere in the midst of all of this change to my meditation practice regimen, I had a breakthrough.

While I was completing the two *ngondro*s I was given, I noticed that at the end of my long, sometimes grueling practice sessions, I was left with the same mind I had all the rest of the time. At the end of these sessions I would do shamatha meditation, and I would find that my mind was still my mind. It's not as if these mantras or physical meditation practices had changed that!

Your mind is your mind is your mind. That is all. If you think a new meditation practice such as mantra recitation or bowing will change that, you are mistaken. When all is said and done, if you are bored with *shamatha* meditation, it is not *shamatha* that is the problem. It is your own inability to be with your mind. It is you that is boring. I recommend training deeply in *shamatha* for years and years before taking on other practices as your primary ones. If you do shift to those practices, do them fully and under the guidance of a qualified teacher.

Contemplation practices and study are good complements to *shamatha*. But *shamatha* can be your bread and butter. You don't need anything else right now. Right now is already perfect. Give *shamatha* a chance.

What Makes for a "Good" Buddhist

My ex-husband insists that I cannot call myself a Buddhist, since I do not meditate daily and am not part of a *sangha*. Are there any particular requirements to identify oneself as a Buddhist? Personally, I think he is *waaaay* too hung up on labels—one reason he's my ex.

At times I wonder why people get so upset about identifying as a Buddhist. This woman's question is a good one, to be sure, but why do you have to label yourself at all? Our friend Sid wasn't a Buddhist. Even when he became enlightened, he did not exclaim, "Now I'm a Buddhist!" He said he was a buddha, or an awakened being. At no point thereafter did he turn to his followers and say, "I want you to make a religious movement based on my identity. Call yourselves "Awakened-one-ists."

Yes, people practice following the Buddha's example. He's a hell of a role model. So if the Buddha were here with us today, instead of weighing in on what it takes to be a Buddhist, I could see him encouraging your meditation practice, mentioning that it is helpful to have spiritual friends with whom you can discuss your practice, and telling you to call yourself whatever you like.

This particular question raises a larger one, namely, "What would make for a 'good' Buddhist?" Would it be going to lots of Buddhist temples? Knowing all the sutras, the words of the Buddha, by heart? Having hundreds of Buddhist meditation practices? I don't think so. Without further ado, here is my top-seven list of things that would make you a good Buddhist—even though I think fixating on terms like *good* and *Buddhist* is counterproductive to just being completely present and releasing yourself from stuck mind.

The seven things to do if you're going to call yourself a good Buddhist—even though I do highly recommend avoiding the label entirely—are as follows:

1. Have a Connection to Mindfulness-Awareness Practice

It's hard to call yourself a Buddhist if you aren't even working with your mind. So it's important to learn *shamatha* meditation, contemplation practices, or other meditation techniques from skilled and authorized teachers within a Buddhist lineage. Obviously, I emphasize *shamathu* in the context of this book, but if you have a connection to a Buddhist tradition that emphasizes bowing or mantra, that is completely valid so long as you are using it as a mindfulness practice and not a cool hobby.

2. Seek Further Awakening and Enlightenment

What's the point in having a meditation practice if you're not trying to change at all? I used to serve as the executive director of a meditation center in Boston. When people came in, they weren't yet seeking enlightenment; they were seeking a way to work with their mind to reduce their own suffering. I think any motivation ranging between wanting to be less mired in confusion and ultimate awakening is damn fine, since it's based on a desire to better oneself.

As Chögyam Trungpa Rinpoche has said, "The practice of meditation is not so much about the hypothetical attainment of enlightenment. It is about leading a good life."[8] So it is a good idea not to get hung up on the large task of attaining nirvana. Maybe to begin with, we should all just start by being kind people. Maybe we should try to live a good and decent life. Enlightenment may very well follow.

3. Learn Something

Study. Study a lot. Read a dharma book. Go receive instruction from great teachers. Listen to a podcast. Watch a video. But meditation without study is like riding a bicycle with one wheel; you're not going to get very far. I am always impressed by the great meditation masters who just exude wisdom and compassion. Even though they are so awake and amazing, they continue to study every day. As the great eleventh-century scholar Sakya Pandita said, "Even if you are going to die tomorrow, you can still learn something tonight." We can take his advice and better ourselves through diligently studying the dharma.

The beauty about dharma is that we can read or hear the same thing over and over again, and because we have changed in the interim, it will meet us in a new way. Some of my favorite dharma books are ones that I have read several dozen times. Each time I read one, I come across an aspect of it and think, "I've never seen that paragraph before." It is not that words were magically inserted into my book but that I am differently receptive to the teachings because of the change in my own experience.

4. Learn from Fellow Practitioners

Just because they're not a group of fully enlightened beings doesn't mean you can't learn a great deal from a *sangha,* or community, of Buddhists. Personally speaking, I've found it essential to have fellow travelers on the path with whom to discuss my experience of meditation practice and debate philosophical topics—and who will call me on my shit.

Sometimes people think the Buddha is a good example to follow, that his teachings are great but that this whole *sangha* thing is tedious. If you think about who is attracted to meditation practice, it is primarily people who have realized they are suffering in some way. So we all have that much in common and can support one another in addressing that topic. Be patient with your *sangha,* and at the very least you can use them as a tool for cultivating compassion.

5. Try Not to Cause Harm

Not causing harm is nice work if you can get it, and you can get it if you try. It does take time and care, though. Often even the most seemingly harmless comments can cause negativity in the minds of those around us. You make a joke about a silly thing your friend did years ago, and she falls suddenly silent for the rest of the night. Only the next day do you check in with her and find out that you ruined her night because you shared such an embarrassing story in front of her crush. If you had been a bit more careful and seen the situation a bit more clearly, you might not have caused her pain. The more we become mindful of our words and actions, the less we find ourselves creating harm in the world.

6. Do Some Good for the World

The Buddha could have sat under the *bodhi* tree content to believe that none of us schmucks would really be able to understand his teachings. Instead he got up and went about trying to lead everyone he encountered toward awakening. Granted, we're not yet buddhas, but beyond trying not to fuck things up in the world around us, we can try to plant some positive seeds.

While a bit corny, I think even just smiling at someone who looks as if she or he is going through hell has a ripple effect not unlike that of the allegorical butterfly's wings' leading to a hurricane. Later in this book we will talk more about social action, but I think each of these chapters is based on the idea that we should be trying to do some good for the world.

7. Last but Not Least, Consider Meditation Practice a Practice for Your Life

It is wonderful to sit on a cushion for a period of time each day or week. However, it doesn't really mean anything unless we consider that we call it practice because we are training ourselves for the twenty-three hours and forty minutes of our day when we are not meditating. We can do any number of outwardly spiritual things to show the world how holy we are, but if we do not take the teachings on wisdom and compassion to heart, then we're just spouting confusion under the label of Buddhism. And that's dumb.

I remember when I was a beginning practitioner I went on a long drive with my mother, someone who had at that point been practicing meditation for more than twenty years. She was speaking negatively about someone, and, frustrated, I turned to her and exclaimed, "How can you say that and still call yourself a Buddhist?"

I feel quite foolish looking back on that incident. I know many Buddhists who are much sloppier with their speech, who begin to drink before noon, who will try to fornicate indiscriminately. Still, I would never deny them the right to call themselves Buddhist, assuming their primary motivation is not to give in to negative habits but to wake up from them. For the record, my mother was quick to point out that while she may have said something negative, I was the one trying to act holy yet was so easily seduced by the strong emotion of anger. Reflecting on that moment continues to remind me that I have a lot of work to do in embodying these teachings and not letting them be just theoretical.

The Buddhist path is that of change through working with your own mind and heart. If you are into that, feel free to call yourself whatever you like. I hope these seven aspects will guide you in determining how you want to manifest as a Buddhist and that you will work to embody the teachings rather than just try to understand them intellectually. Whether you decide to call yourself a Buddhist or not, the important thing is that you are trying to wake up.

FINDING A COMMUNITY

There are so many different Buddhist lineages and traditions! Of course, they are the result of different cultural contexts and historical circumstances, and each is its own unique expression of the dharma. In many ways it's wonderful that there are such varieties. But it can also be confusing. If I'm interested in practicing Buddhism, how do I know which tradition to choose? How can I separate bogus teachings from the real thing?

While the Buddha's teachings may have originated in India, they have since spread throughout the world. Not unlike Christianity, as the doctrine took root in various countries, it would change and adapt to meet the cultural norms of the times. Thus, Buddhism in Thailand looks very different from Buddhism in Tibet. Even specific schools of Buddhism, such as Zen, look completely different from one another in countries such as Korea and Japan.

As the Buddha's teachings moved to new lands, it is not that the teachings themselves were diluted or thrown out but that the specific tenets within the tradition were modified so that they would be appropriate for the time and place the teachings were being received. That is why many contemporary teachers attempt to apply meditation to today's world, where there is constant ad bombardment, where the Internet exists, and where we have larger weapons for destruction of both each other and Mother Earth. The Buddha was not around to address specifically how to relate mindfully to our contemporary society, but he did lay out teachings that we can study, reflect on, and apply to our modern-day lives.

That being said, we live in unique times. In the United States alone, in the short span of less than a century, we have had the wonderful fortune of hosting teachers and meditation centers from every Buddhist tradition around the globe. Think about that for a minute: whereas a few hundred years ago very few people would know the differences between Tibetan Buddhism and Japanese Zen, today you can walk around New York City and, in the span of an hour, experience both.

Recently I visited Sacramento to lead a few workshops. One group I visited was an inter-Buddhist group. Not interfaith or interreligious but inter-Buddhist, meaning that they were a group that met to sit meditation together once a week but also belonged to a dozen different *sanghas,* or communities, around the city. One person raised his hand and asked something similar to this question: "How do I know which *sangha* to choose?"

At first my mind went to a scene in the television show *Arrested Development,* where the patriarch of the family has ended up in jail and is being courted for membership by all of the gangs in prison. At one point he looks to his son and softly says, "I feel like the prettiest girl at the dance."

I believe that exploring various Buddhist communities can sometimes feel that way. Each group wants to be receptive. They want you to walk in and feel comfortable there. They want you to enjoy your time there so that, ideally, you will feel encouraged in your meditation practice. They are not going to show you their ugly underbelly in your initial visit. "Let me introduce you to one of our senior students, Chris. He's an alcoholic who might hit on you." That just doesn't happen.

Instead of quoting *Arrested Development* though, I responded to this woman's question by talking a little bit about intuition. When you meditate, it is a bit like peeling an onion. When you meditate you sit there, and while it doesn't look like you are doing anything, you are in fact getting to know your mind very well. You are exploring your own quirks, habitual patterns, and neuroses to the point that you may be able to shuck some of those aspects like you would shuck one layer of an onion. Because you continually come back to the breath on the meditation cushion, it is a bit as if you were taking a tiny sharp knife to your confusion, peeling off layers of it.

You sit on the cushion, and a major emotional upheaval pops into your mind: "I can't believe she left me. Why? What did I do?" Ideally, you acknowledge that thought and come back to the breath. Maybe it comes up over and over again. Maybe you come back to your breath over and over again. Over time the neurosis around "I'm not good enough" or "Here's where I messed up" starts to fade away. You are taking the knife of meditation and shucking off those layers of external confusion the same way you might shuck further layers from the onion. You have to realize that the layers may be very thin. You may not notice that you are doing it, that another layer has slowly slipped off. But you are more able just to be with your breathing.

A funny thing about that process: the more you are able to take the knife of meditation to your confusion, the more you reveal what is underneath. At the core under our neuroses is basic goodness. When you are in tune with your basic goodness, it is like having a little voice whisper in your ear, guiding you toward virtuous activity. It is an instrument of discernment, letting you know whether a particular job opportunity or romantic idea is right for you. It is the compass for your intuition.

I often encourage people to explore as many different Buddhist communities as they can. I myself was raised within the Shambhala tradition but took the time to explore other religious traditions and then a number of lineages within Buddhism before coming back and understanding that Shambhala is where I feel most at home.

The idea of coming home in this sense is not about going to the Buddhist organization that most encourages you to kick back and put your feet up. It is about getting to know a community of practitioners, hearing the dharma with an open mind, and seeing if it lands in your heart. The Buddha is said to have been approached by his former colleagues shortly after his enlightenment. They wanted him to teach them how to be exactly like him. Before the Buddha uttered a word of teachings, he issued an invitation: "Come and see for yourself."

We have to see for ourselves what of the Buddha's words feels like home to us. If you cannot see the truth of the teachings in your own experience, then do not follow them. Buddhism is not a tradition of blindly doing what others say you ought to do. While I wouldn't call another person's sangha bogus, I do think any group that tries to convince you that it is the best, that you should blindly trust the group, may be worth serious scrutiny. It's about testing the mettle of the dharma and seeing how it applies to your life.

As you get to know the various Buddhist communities you are attracted to, listen to your intuition. Try to be as present as you can and connect with your own basic goodness. See how you are guided by the teachers and *sangha*s at these locations and whether you think you will be able to receive the dharma genuinely in any given space. If not, don't go there. If so, then that is likely the *sangha* for you.

Mistakes Are the Fodder for Our Journey

How would Sid deal with lack of skillfulness when he blunders or makes a mistake? I often experience chagrin and shame, disappointment. I must have a harsh inner critic that is tenacious or something.

We all make mistakes. We all have regrets. One of my favorite haikus, by the late poet Masajo Suzuki, reads,

is life possible
without regret?
the beer foams over . . .[9]

Even the historical Buddha had a period when he made the mistake of overcompensating for his luxurious upbringing by becoming an ascetic and starving himself. He tortured himself under the name of spirituality. That's a big mistake. However, he would not have been able to find the middle way between the extremes of luxury and asceticism if he had not experienced both as something other than his cup of tea. In other words, mistakes are not a bad thing; they are the fodder for our spiritual journey.

We each have our go-to emotion when we make a mistake. Yours could be shame or disappointment. Other people may get defensive. Yet others try to place blame on anyone but themselves.

The first thing we can do when we make a mistake is take a long, honest look at what happened. What factors brought you to the point where you made it? Were you speedy? Arrogant? What emotional and mental path took you to the point where you made such a blunder? Once you have figured that out, you can resolve not to make such an error again. Making the same mistake after resolving not to would be like walking backward down the spiritual path. It is also a sign that your regret was likely not genuine.

Sometimes when you make a mistake, you might feel that there are many other people to blame. For example, someone from work sees you acting the fool over the weekend with some friends, blows the whole story out of proportion, spreads it around, and the next thing you know, the boss is looking at you funny come Monday morning. You could blame your coworker (and heck, that's easy to do), but you also have to realize that if you weren't acting foolish in the first place, there would be no story.

The eleventh-century meditation master and teacher Atisha is known for composing a series of pithy *lojong*, or mind-training, slogans. One of these slogans is "Drive all blames into one." Quite simply put, this slogan refers to the fact that instead of looking to external factors as the source of our mistakes, we need to own up to our experience. As Chögyam Trungpa Rinpoche wrote in his book *Training the Mind and Cultivating Loving-Kindness:*

"We could blame the organization; we could blame the government; we could blame the police force; we could blame the weather; we could blame the food; we could blame the highways; we could blame our own motorcars, our own clothes; we could blame an infinite variety of things. But it is we who are not letting go, not developing enough warmth and sympathy—which makes us problematic. So we cannot blame anybody."[10]

When we make mistakes, we often develop a sense of rigidity about ourselves. We come down hard either on ourselves or on others. We start blaming an amorphous "they" who ruin everything all the time. This is not helpful.

Instead, if you can look to your role in your mistakes, you can honestly see how to avoid them in the future. You can apply a gentle attitude to your exploration, suspending judgment about what a jerk you are. You can develop warmth and have some sympathy for yourself. Then you can acknowledge what you did and resolve not to do it again.

Furthermore, you can offset the negative actions you have done in the past by producing positive ones now. It may not be a one-to-one equation, where you take your coworkers out for pizza so that they think you're a swell guy or gal. In fact, it may not be related to your mistake at all. However, you can use the knowledge that you have caused some form of harm as fuel for trying to cause some good in this world.

Over time, mistakes fade and people mature. Because we have all made mistakes, we all know that at some point we must forgive those of others. If you genuinely acknowledge your errors and work to produce positive actions, people will pick up on that. No one remembers the Buddha as someone who made mistakes; they only remember his incredible kindness and wisdom. Even though we make mistakes today, if we endeavor to learn from them, then we too will be remembered in the same light.

DATING YOUR MIND

Do I really have to meditate every day? What if I don't want to meditate; can I still benefit by just reading dharma books?

Meditation is a bit like dating your mind. At first you try it out; you go on a first date when you sit down to receive initial meditation instruction. After that you have one of three responses:

I like it and want to do this again; I hate it and am going to try to avoid my mind at all costs; or, it's okay, I guess maybe spending time with my mind will grow on me.

Assuming you and your mind make it past the first date, you start to see each other here and there. You and your mind get together at your favorite date spot, the meditation cushion, and you engage in your favorite activity, which is being present with the breath. Sure, sometimes your mind gets distracted. Sometimes you get annoyed at it. But you know you want to do this thing, so you persevere past the upsets.

Over time you might see your mind by meditating more regularly. At first you and your mind were just getting together once or twice a week, but you have become accustomed to each other. You are befriending your mind. You want to spend more time together, so you are sitting on the cushion longer and more frequently.

The idea of meditating every day is that you are settling down with your mind. You are making this relationship a priority, just as you would a steady girlfriend or boyfriend. When you go a day without spending time with your mind, it feels awkward and uncomfortable. You long to get to the cushion and hang out with yourself. So, to answer the first half of this question, no you don't *have* to meditate every day. No one will unsubscribe you from *Good Buddhist* magazine if you miss a day of meditation here or there. But you might find that you want to sit every day, and that's okay too.

As for the second half of this question, as you start to get serious with your mind, you might want to take it out on the town. The meditation cushion is great, but you go there all the time. It's time to take it out to a good dharma book. There are so many, and in the resources at the back of this book you will find a list of some of my favorites.

One thing you can do is leave one book near where you meditate and another by your bed. You might want to pick up the former and read for a few minutes before or after your regular meditation session. This could allow you a chance to ease into your practice or give you advice on how to approach your life postmeditation. You might want to pick up the latter right as you wake up or as you are about to go to sleep. Reading even just one chapter during these times helps you transition in and out of your day.

One thing I would recommend, though, is taking your mind out to a *lot* of good dharma books. If variety is the spice of life, then keep your relationship with your mind hot and juicy by learning as much as you can about the teachings. When you marry your meditation practice to your dharma study, you will progress along the path much more fluidly than if you do only one or the other.

To give a more direct answer to the second half of the question, you can always benefit from reading the dharma. But you might fall into the trap of its just becoming theoretical nonsense if you do not meditate as well. By meditating you are taking your mind to what you are reading about, and it enjoys that. Just reading the dharma is like talking a lot about getting into a relationship. Meditation is taking the big plunge and going out to dinner: take your mind to dinner, and for dessert read a good dharma book.

Getting a Practice Going

What are some suggestions for maintaining the practice of meditation at home?

Meditation is not a hobby. You can treat it like a hobby, but if you do you are sort of missing the point. It is, in fact, a tool that can help us transform into kinder, gentler, more compassionate and aware people. But I want to issue a disclaimer: if you are not interested in changing as a person, don't meditate.

Meditation is something that changes you, thankfully for the better. It highlights your habitual patterns and neuroses and gives you a chance not to engage in that activity so much. It gives you space in your life so you can approach your world with a fresh perspective. It offers you an opportunity to be more present with your world and realize just how sacred it can be. Chöygam Trungpa Rinpoche once said, "Sacredness is not just an idea. It is an experience. Having a realization of sacredness means that you experience an element of power and dignity in everything, including the ballpoint pen you are using, your comb, taking a shower, or driving your car."[11]

If you are into all of that, then you need to have a regular meditation practice. There is no way around it. If you want to treat it like a hobby, meditate once a month or so. I promise there is no harm done by doing that. However, if you want to engage in a process of inner transformation, then you ought to aim to sit meditation several times a week, ideally daily.

The first suggestion I would offer in terms of getting a regular meditation practice going in your home is making space for it, both physically and mentally. Physically, that means clearing out an area in your home where you can set up a consistent meditation practice. If you want, you can buy a meditation cushion (see the resources section of this book for suggestions on that).

Having a meditation cushion in your house is like having a mute yet nagging mother. You know your mother really thinks you ought to do certain things, like eat better or meet a nice person to date, and while she is always there in your life, she can't say anything about it because, well, she's mute. A meditation cushion can play the same role if you place it somewhere obvious in your home. You will walk by it, and while it can't talk, it will indicate to you, "Didn't you mean to sit on me today?" You will have a slight wave of guilt (drop that please— that's not helping anyone), but after walking by it a few times, you will acquiesce and do what you already know is good for you: meditate.

If you don't want to buy a meditation cushion, you can take the pillow from your bed or a couch cushion. However, those objects aren't dedicated to reminding you to meditate, so perhaps you should put something else in your home that will serve that function. That could be a statue of the Buddha, a small painting or picture of him or a Buddhist teacher you admire, or even just an incense holder or candle. Having that designated physical space in your home will serve as a regular reminder that you have made a personal commitment to yourself to maintain a meditation practice.

In terms of making space for meditation mentally, the best thing to do is set up a consistent time that you meditate. Some people like to meditate first thing in the morning, when they wake up, while others like to do it after work or before bed. I myself will wake up, do a little bit of work, and then meditate in the morning before I launch fully into my day.

My friend Eric recently told me about how he has made a conscious choice to meditate in the morning. When he gets out of bed, he walks down the hall and has two options: if he turns left he enters his meditation room. If he turns right he enters his office and gets down to work. Eric is a very busy man, so once he has made that choice to begin work, he will be yanked around all day until he collapses at night exhausted, too tired to meditate. So he has committed to a specific act every morning: turn left.

In fact, he and a few friends support one another's meditation practice based on this idea. They e-mail the group every day, letting the others know when they "turn left" and practice. Even though the others don't live in my friend's apartment, the principle still applies, and it is nice that they remind one another to practice each day.

In addition to designating a consistent time of day that you reserve as your meditation period, I recommend being consistent in the length of time you meditate. For a beginner, it makes sense to start at ten minutes a day, maybe working your way toward twenty. Some days that will feel like a lot, while on others when your timer goes off you might feel as if you just sat down. Both are good. It's important to remain gentle with yourself as you start your meditation practice. No one is going to give you a slap on the back and congratulate you for being hard on yourself. So don't label your meditation sessions as good or bad. Any time you meditate is good meditation.

I have read that if you want to create a new habit, you need to do something for twenty-one days straight. If you are trying to write, try writing a little bit for twenty-one days and see if you form a habit for that. If you are looking to stop smoking, aim to stop for twenty-one days and see if you have an easier time quitting after that length of time. In terms of meditation, I think that's a good rule. If you are serious about starting a practice, aim to do it for twenty-one days in a row. If you skip one by accident, that's okay. But try to do a full twenty-one.

After that you will likely see the effects of meditation and want to continue to do it. That is wonderful. At that point you should assess your life and set realistic goals for how and when you will meditate. You might have very busy weekends, so you know that you will most likely meditate Monday through Friday at a certain time. Or maybe you work nights and get up later in the day, so that you want to sit at 1:00 p.m. seven days a week. The important thing is that you make this meditation practice personal and make it your own. From there you will see the fruits of your labor and will be able to be fully there for yourself and everyone you encounter.

2 / PLAY LIKE A BUDDHA

Meditation is not something that you just do to do it. You engage meditation practice as a means for living your life with mindfulness and compassion. The people I often talk to, though, aren't chaste monastics who live quiet lives. They are ambitious businesspeople, party-hardy students, serial daters, and passionate activists. They want to practice meditation but do not want to throw out these other aspects of their lives. Thankfully, they don't have to.

In this chapter we explore how to get off the meditation cushion, go to the bar or the party or the tattoo parlor, and still maintain our mindfulness. I try to refrain from strict judgment on these topics and encourage you to do so as well.

I was once asked by a reporter about why I talk about drinking in my Buddhist writing. "If teenagers are going to have sex," I replied, "do you think it's more effective to tell them not to do it or to educate them on how to be safe?" The same logic goes into my thoughts on going out. If you are going to go out and smoke or do drugs or if you're going to spend hours on Facebook, at least do it with Buddhist principles in mind. No pressure to do any of these things (life would likely be simpler if you didn't), but if you're going to, here's how to bring your meditation practice to bear in these situations.

Right Drinking

> One of the five precepts the Buddha laid out to monastics is that they should not partake of alcohol or other intoxicants. I'm not a monk though. I like to drink occasionally. Does this precept then mean that I can't go on a bender? Or that I can drink as much as I like as long as I remain mindful?

When the Buddha attracted a number of followers interested in pursuing the path of meditation, he realized he needed to lay down some ground rules. Principal among them were the precepts, including the idea that his monastic followers should not take life, steal, engage in sexual misconduct, use mindless speech, or take intoxicants. This fifth precept was *surā-meraya-majja-pamādaṭṭhānā veramaṇī sikkhāpadaṃ samādiyāmi*, or "I undertake the training rule of abstaining from intoxicants that cause heedlessness."

Most Buddhist teachers stick pretty strongly to the whole "I undertake the vow to abstain from intoxicants that cause heedlessness" precept. However, traditional monastic systems often clash with the reality of a modern existence in the West. I know a number of Buddhists who drink—and others who do not drink—based on what level of heedlessness they think they can avoid. As such we need to determine for ourselves what it means to partake in intoxicants that can easily lead to confusion and recklessness.

The first question I might pose to any meditator would be, "Do you actually want to drink, or do you feel societal pressure to do so?" If you feel that you can't be a meditation practitioner who drinks, that's fine. If you think you're only going to the bar because that's where your friends hang out, that might be something worth examining.

However, it seems that this question is not so much "Is it okay to drink?" but "How can I drink while not losing my head?" That is a great question for any meditator in today's world who is a lay practitioner and doesn't want to cut alcohol out of his or her life completely. How often have you seen an alcohol ad that ended with "Drink responsibly"? What does that even mean? The alcohol companies aren't going to tell us, so we have to figure it out for ourselves.

Personally, I feel that when we're trying to bring our mindfulness off the meditation cushion and into our everyday world, we can't say, "I'll be mindful washing the dishes, at work, walking the dog, but not when I drink." If you want to lead a mindful life, then you should aim to have meditation practice penetrate every aspect of your existence. It cannot be something you apply just to certain occasions—it is a tool for relating with every aspect of who you are and what you do.

Early on in his teaching career, the Buddha laid out what is known as the Eightfold Path. It includes principles for living a good life, such as engaging in right livelihood or right speech. I have always wondered: If there is right speech, why can't the modern-day practitioner engage in right drinking?

Let's take a look at a snapshot history behind alcohol and Buddhism. It starts with Siddhartha drinking regularly in his youth, likely without much sense of mindfulness. Later on, when he became a buddha, he acknowledged that alcohol is a dangerous fire to play with and laid out the precept for his monastic followers. Over time, as Buddhism spread and encountered new lands, it morphed to accommodate those cultures. Today in many monasteries in Tibet and India, Vajrayana practitioners will incorporate alcohol as part of their practice.

The intent is not to get the monks schwasted but to take what is seen as a poison and transform it into a tool for spaciousness. Chögyam Trungpa Rinpoche attempted to lead his advanced Vajrayana students in the West in what he referred to as "mindful drinking," with mixed results. Some students would engage the practice to the point where they felt a loosening up of their ego and their dualistic sense of "me" versus "the world." Others threw up.

One student of Chögyam Trungpa Rinpoche's said they

were encouraged to "drink just enough to relax, to appreciate your situation, and to help your ego go to sleep." The idea was to watch how the alcohol affects you and see how it can relax your mind. When you feel that loosening inside you, then you stop.

Unfortunately, most of us don't stop there. Most of us go out with the intention of loosening our mind, celebrating something with friends, or having a low-key get-together and then don't have the discipline to say no to one more drink. That is the moment when we break with not just the letter but the spirit of the precepts: we end up causing harm to ourselves or others.

With that said, I think right drinking is a practice modern-day meditators could engage in. If you're going to drink, you really do need to drink responsibly. To start, this practice could include the following:

Know Your Intention

It is important to know your intention in all things. Are you motivated to drink as a practice tool? To shake off a bad day at work? To relax with a friend? To wash your sorrows away? Knowing in advance what you're intending to use alcohol for is important. Drinking alcohol is a bit like taking out a chain saw; if you don't know what you intend to do with it, you're going to get hurt. So check yourself before you wreck yourself.

Taste It

Tasting practice is a very simple way to bring mindfulness to your drinking habits. Don't chug your drink, don't gulp it down, but try to taste every sip. Enjoy the alcohol you drink. Along those lines, I'd recommend drinking less and drinking good alcohol. Quality not quantity. Slowing down physically allows you to maintain your mindfulness as you engage this dangerous substance.

Watch What Happens to Your Mind

Notice the effect the alcohol has on you. You don't have to make a big deal of it, closing your eyes and doing a ten-minute body scan or anything, but you can at least pause after you finish a drink, look up, rest your mind, and see how you feel. See when you start to become less mindful with your speech or gestures or with the person you're making out with.

Find Your Own Middle Way

It might be that you're walking the fine line of relaxed, spacious, and pleasant now, but will one more drink push you over the edge into crazy town? As Chögyam Trungpa Rinpoche encouraged his students to do, stop while you can still appreciate the situation. This is often a trial-and-error process, but over time you can find a way and an amount to drink that feels right to you.

Alcohol is easy to abuse. I don't want it to seem that I'm trying to make binge drinking okay by saying it is meditation. That's the opposite of what I'm trying to get across. Instead, I'm saying that if we're going to engage in this type of activity, let's bring mindfulness to the act of drinking. Let's not overindulge but work with our craving for alcohol in a fashion similar to the way we work with craving on the meditation cushion. If you engage your nights out with mindfulness and play it safe, don't be surprised at the end of the night if instead of feeling woozy you feel refreshed by the experience.

SMOKING CIGARETTES

> I've started meditating lately and studying the Hinayana view of Buddhism. It seems that a lot of that view is about taking care of yourself and not causing harm. I'm a longtime cigarette smoker—am I breaking from the Hinayana teachings if I continue to smoke?

The term *hinayana* has been translated sometimes as "narrow vehicle" as opposed to the more derogatory "lesser vehicle." I like the term *narrow vehicle* better because the connotation is that you are starting to narrow your focus and look at your own shit. It's very simple: we are getting our act together and trying to be kind to ourselves and others. In that sense, its ramifications are anything but narrow! I reply to the question using this term with the utmost respect for the idea of narrowing in on how we can change ourselves for the better in order to become awake.

The basic principle involved in the Hinayana path is developing trust in your own buddha nature through cultivating mindfulness on and off the meditation cushion. Part of this path is taking a hard look at your own life and discerning which aspects of your normal way of doing things are helping you wake up and which are not. Kindness is not just about how you treat others; it's rooted in being gentle to yourself.

To cut to the chase, I would recommend asking yourself, "Does smoking regularly cause me harm?" From a practical point of view, inhaling smoke for ten minutes at a time, ten or twenty times a day, does cause your body physical harm. You don't need me or the teachings of the Buddha to tell you that; you likely know it already.

Now let's look at the other side of this activity—is it harmful to your mental state? You can analyze whether you have an addiction to smoking or whether it's a casual thing, something you enjoy once a week, and so on. Look at your motivation for smoking. From this exploration you can determine whether smoking has become a habit that is not helping you get your shit together.

Obviously, it's not as simple as saying, "Gee, I guess this isn't helping me in my goals in life. I'll just stop." If you are a longtime smoker, it's not easy. My father is a meditation practitioner who smoked for twenty-plus years. When he finally decided to quit, he took his last cigarette and placed it in a covered glass butter dish on his desk. He practiced incredible discipline. It has sat there for twenty more years, in plain sight, but he never smoked that cigarette or any other cigarette again. Since he has retired, it now sits on a shelf in his apartment.

The reason he was able to maintain his discipline is that he had already studied in-depth his personal relationship to smoking. He had taken a long hard look at the craving he felt and recognized it as an addiction. From a mental point of view, he realized that giving in to the craving for a cigarette was causing him harm. That was a good motivational factor to help him quit.

When you apply the practice of mindfulness meditation to your life, you are, in essence, learning to cut through the habitual way you have done things in the past. You are learning to see what harmful desires might arise, including all the various ways you cause pain to your own body and mind.

If you feel that you should continue to smoke, continue to smoke. I'm not going to come to your house and throw your pack away. That would be me getting hooked by my own fixed views and opinions, which are often referred to as *shenpa*. *Shenpa* can be translated from Tibetan as "attachment," but more specifically it is a sharp, sticky form of attachment. It is when a strong emotion or fixed view gets its hooks into us and we act out because of that.

Pema Chödrön once commented on the topic of smoking. She said that, in essence, smoking is just smoking. She said this knowing that some people might come down on her for not taking a hard stance against it, citing long studies about how smoking is a health hazard and how it produces lung cancer. She said, "Consider the vehemence with which you oppose the idea that smoking is just smoking, or the vehemence with which you support it. Smoking may not be intrinsically right or wrong, but it certainly stirs up a lot of shenpa."[1]

When we get hooked by fixed opinions, for or against anything, we are bound to create suffering for ourselves and others. That is why I always encourage people to find out for themselves how the Buddha's principles apply to their lives. It is very personal.

If you agree that smoking is having a negative effect on you, then you should rejoice in that discovery. Having discerned that you are causing yourself harm, you can resolve not to give in to craving. Instead, when you notice the craving to smoke arise, you can stay with it without acting on it, just as you do with any powerful fantasy or emotion on the meditation cushion. You can hold your seat and recognize that you are not powerless over this strong habitual force in your life. You can remain present with it and over time ingrain new habits that you feel good about.

FOMO AND COOL BOREDOM

> How would a Buddhist handle the "fear of missing out?" When Friday night hits, there is always this nagging feeling that it's time to let loose a bit . . . even though my "innate wisdom" always tells me going to clubs or crowded bars is not going to make me happy. But there is still always that "you better do it now or you'll regret you passed it up on Monday" feeling.

We live in a society that has pretty warped notions of what it means to have a good time. At one point Chögyam Trungpa Rinpoche described going out as an experience where you go to "very dark dungeons with bad lighting, where you get drunk." He was referring to nightclubs. More often than not, this is a pretty apt description. Yet for so many people it is the perfect place to go to escape from whatever horrors the work week brought you.

If you take an escapist view of going out on the town, then you will end up disappointed. If you think that drinking a lot or doing drugs or grinding on some stranger will bring you a lasting sense of happiness, you should give it a go. See how that works out for you. Sometimes doing those things, while in the company of good friends and in moderation, might bring a temporary sense of joy. More often than not you wake up the next day exhausted and hungover. Whatever you attempted to escape from is waiting at the foot of your bed, bigger and badder now that you're at your worst. Trust me, I know.

The difference for me has, over time, become that I am not fooling myself into thinking those activities will erase any of the pain or difficulty in my life. They are distractions, not unlike Facebook or online shopping. They may be fun to engage in but are not going to bring me true contentment or move me closer to waking up to my basic nature.

If your inner voice, your intuition, makes you feel that you don't want to play in that scene, don't go there. There are so many other ways to connect with friends: you can get together for dinner or go for a walk or exercise together. Back when we were younger, my friend Oliver and I would play tennis every Sunday. I am horrible at tennis, but it was a time when we could connect, catch up, and still do something healthy. I never felt that I was missing out on something; I was content with appreciating my friend in a very basic way.

However, the idea of fomo, or fear of missing out, is based not in discerning how you want to spend your time but in fear that you are not doing a good job of doing so. Fear is a powerful motivator in all of our lives. It prevents us from realizing what is going on in the present. We get lost in worrying about the future. That sense of worry is not based on reality. It is based on our own internal story line.

In this case, the story line might look something like this: "All of my friends are going to have these shared experiences, and I will never get their inside jokes" or "Maybe tonight is the night I will finally meet the love of my life; if I don't go I'll end up alone forever" or just "If I don't go out I am a loser." These are all fear-based reactions; we don't have to give in to them. Meditation allows us to come back to the reality of the situation at hand. In this current moment there are no story lines. There is only possibility.

Chögyam Trungpa Rinpoche has said that meditation practice is a method to relate to what he called cool boredom.

Cool boredom is the experience of just being with what is, as opposed to what we are scared we might be missing out on. It is anti-fomo. Trungpa said, "It refreshes because we do not have to do anything or expect anything."[2] Pema Chödrön has described this experience as a carefree, spacious feeling where we don't need to seek entertainment at all. In this moment we can find contentment. We can realize that something very perfect is happening right now. If you are able to do that, then you can overcome your fear. When you drop fear and just be, you miss out on nothing at all.

DRUGS AND ADDICTION

> What would you say about someone who is living a successful life and using drugs regularly, as a habit? This person smokes pot daily and occasionally takes other types of drugs. But this person's life is going pretty well, he's not majorly fucking up or anything. Also, what is the Buddhist take on psychedelics? I'm clearly asking for a friend.

Here's my deductive reasoning on the topic of drugs: the Buddha based his teachings on the truths he discovered through his experience. He also said that intoxicants lead to carelessness and should be avoided. So I'm led to believe Siddhartha must have gotten tipsy or high from time to time on the local flavor twenty-six hundred years ago. Thus, he knew that these intoxicants aren't helpful to one's path. Some of us may feel the need to follow in his footsteps and see if that's true for us too.

So from one perspective, yeah, drugs are not a great way to go. They can send you on crazy trips that are not based on reality. They can soak up the serotonin levels in your brain and lead you to feel depressed. They can trick you into dumb-ass shit. It's hard to maintain one's mindfulness when the world is breathing colors. But it is up to you to figure whether drugs and Buddhism mix.

I do want to note that the question here is not just "what about drugs" but "what about using drugs regularly." We all have addictions. It can be something classic, like weed or alcohol; or something more socially accepted, like drinking coffee every morning; or even subtle, such as being addicted to checking Facebook constantly. Addiction is a tricky thing, and the first thing someone who is interested in this question can do is explore whether what is being called a habit is an addiction.

If it is indeed addiction, I believe it is best to seek professional help through Narcotics Anonymous or a rehab facility. Meditation is wonderful as a habit-breaking activity, but for physical addiction, I like to think of it as more of a complement to traditional methods than a replacement for them. There are a number of Buddhist and non-Buddhist AA and NA groups around the country that address this topic more fully.

However, if you are the sort of person who likes to indulge in a bit of weed here and there but have not formed a reliance on it, you could move on to the next step: stay vigilant. I have known incredibly charming, lovely alcoholics and druggies who have strung together lucky chance after lucky chance to have a nice life. Some are extremely high functioning, despite ingesting an incredible amount of intoxicants. Eventually, though, the house of cards has come crashing down and those individuals have realized they couldn't have it all. Continue to monitor your intake and be inquisitive when it comes to your relationship to substances. You run the risk of getting bit in the ass when it's too late.

As with so many of these tricky areas, it is important to know your own intention and get your priorities straight. Are you trying to coast by through life or are you trying to make a difference in the world? To use the phrase from the initial question, just because you're not majorly fucking up doesn't mean you are living a life of mindfulness and compassion. There are, of course, a million shades of gray in between. So if you use drugs, see if your usage is in line with your overall priorities in life.

If you are committed to living your life in a way connected to your own meditation practice, I have to ask: Does your habit keep you grounded and awake to the world around you? Or does it layer you in protective goggles, distancing you from reality? As always, no judgment from my end; this is something you need to determine for yourself.

In regard to psychedelic drugs, I'm often asked if the trips people experience on them are something akin to enlightenment. Since I'm not enlightened, I can't provide definitive knowledge on this topic, but according to the teachers I have studied with, these impermanent experiences are interesting but not the real deal. Dzongsar Khyentse Rinpoche once said, "A drug cannot provide total awakening, if only because this awakening is dependent on an external substance and when the effect of the [drug] is gone, the experience is gone as well."[3] At most, doing a drug might open your mind in a fresh way, but as Dzongsar Rinpoche points out, it is a transitory experience.

My recommendation, if you do these sorts of drugs and you think you're having some kind of experience, is to acknowledge it, see it for what it is, and come back to the present moment. More often than not, people get all excited that they're experiencing something other than their humdrum life while on drugs and want to solidify that experience into something fixed and real. It's not real. It's the drugs. So don't get too attached. Also, I wouldn't recommend considering your temporary experience to be a deep spiritual achievement; you didn't do much to achieve it besides put mushrooms in your mouth and not throw up a half hour later.

Earlier I mentioned one quality that develops through meditation practice: discernment. Through the practice of meditation you begin to learn more about yourself. You see some patterns that coincide with how you want to live your life. Those are the ones you want to cultivate. Eventually, other patterns that you hadn't thought much about are suddenly spotted as sources of discontent. Those you want to steer away from. Out of this ability to discern what aspects of yourself you want to accept versus what you might want to reject or cut out, you can align your lifestyle with the moral compass of your heart.

On one hand, taking drugs can be seen as counter to engaging reality as it is, so I can't imagine the Buddha's being a big fan of hitting the pipe on the regular. On the other hand, there are some religious traditions that incorporate drugs as part of waking up. It's up to you to determine whether your habits are helpful or hurtful to the way you want to live your life.

I myself find drugs to be somewhat escapist, so I can't see myself relying on them on a regular basis; I think they would distract me from some of the good work I try to do. I think it would hurt my intention to be more present with the people I interact with every day and to be openhearted with the various obstacles that come up in my life. Maybe for you it's the opposite and your drug habit grounds you right smack in the middle of how you want to live your life.

One more piece of caution: Buddhism is a path that gives us tools to relate with our mind in a way that does not indulge our attachments. As we start to examine our life, we realize that we cannot take refuge in drugs or alcohol any more than we can take refuge in our job, our lover, or our religious identity. If you think any of these things will bring you everlasting comfort, you are sadly mistaken. The important thing, to reiterate, is to remain inquisitive and vigilant about your drug use. See if it helps support you in your endeavors. If not, lay off it.

What about Prescription Drugs?

I have suffered most of my life from bipolar disorder, and it can lead to psychosis because of going for extended periods without sleep. I have followed Buddhism as much as possible in seeking relief from this condition. I now take something that allows sleep. What's the Buddhist view on taking drugs that are prescribed?

As Buddhism has traveled to new lands and cultures, the fifth precept has been interpreted a number of ways. For those individuals interested in observing the five basic precepts today as a layperson, it may mean "no alcohol or drugs." Some people choose to abstain from any substance that causes heedlessness, such as caffeinated beverages. Other people continue to take intoxicants but are careful about whether or not they can cope with the "heedlessness" part, striving not to cause harm to themselves or others as a result of their imbibing.

I realize that some Buddhist teachers may discourage taking prescription drugs, citing this fifth precept. I am going to go out on a limb and disagree with those individuals. I believe that if he were alive today, the Buddha would encourage people with mental-health issues to go ahead and take drugs if that is what is most helpful for them in treating the chemical imbalance in their brains.

What we are talking about here is not an issue of drug abuse but one that seems to fall within the Hinayana perspective of taking care of yourself. In fact, it might be more helpful for people who take prescriptions not to view their situation as being treated by drugs but instead see that they are taking medicine to aid their mind. If you have a chemical imbalance in the brain and there is medicine to help you, then I can't imagine the Buddha's going on at length delivering a "don't help yourself, continue to suffer your chemical imbalance" sutra.

At times I have heard Buddhist teachers say meditation can treat mental disorders. While I think meditation can be an aid to working with strong emotions, I have not found much proof of its curing mental illness. Bipolar disorder is a real thing. My understanding of it is that when you are high, it is different from just being excited, and when you are low, it is different from just feeling sad.

If you are just excited or sad, there are a number of ways to relate to those emotions on the meditation cushion. You can drop the story line that surrounds the feeling and just rest with it. You can contemplate where that emotion exists in your body. You can look at the impermanent nature of emotions. However, if you are clinically depressed, then perhaps you don't just meditate but medicate.

Sakyong Mipham Rinpoche has often said that it is helpful to know when you are and are not able to meditate. Sometimes you may be able to keep coming back to the breath. Other times you may want to contemplate the nature of the emotion. In extreme times maybe meditation isn't the most helpful thing for you. Maybe going for a walk or having a cup of tea would soothe you to the point where you can sit down and relate more fully to your mind and experience.

Obviously, you can give it a go and see if working with your breath is a possibility. However, if you sit down on the meditation cushion and can't even find your breath, then you will spend your whole session just getting frustrated. I truly believe that meditation practice should be enjoyable, not a chore. Part of keeping it enjoyable is knowing when you are capable of practicing.

For anyone dealing with mental-health issues, I would recommend working with your disorder to the best of your ability, and when you feel able, come to the meditation cushion. I would no sooner fault someone for taking his or her prescription to treat bipolar disorder than I would fault someone who was bleeding profusely for getting a bandage before attempting to take a seat on the cushion. In all things, please take care of yourself.

LOOKING DAPPER

I like to wear nice clothes and flamboyant hats. Is that too outrageous: to want to dress well and still be a Buddhist?

There is a saying that "clothes make the man." I think it is perfectly fine to take pride in how you look, but I'm a firm believer that the (hu)man makes the clothes. You don't need to spend a lot of money to look good; looking good comes from radiating your own innate dignity and splendor.

In today's world, we are constantly bombarded by the idea that if you want to be successful, you need to spend lots of money on clothes, makeup, and accessories. That is simply not the case. Success means different things to different people, but even from a conventional worldly point of view you don't have to drop your paycheck on a suit to get ahead in life.

From a Buddhist point of view, success means being awake to what is, without our conventional filter that breaks the world down into three categories: what we like, what we don't like, and what we can get away with ignoring. Success is being able to be present with what is happening in this moment without giving in to our habitual responses of how things should be or once were. Success is being fully in touch with our basic goodness, that deep well of awakened energy we all possess.

The more you meditate, the more present you are to letting this basic goodness radiate out. It is as if we had this brilliant sun within us, eager to permeate all aspects of our life, making us kinder and more peaceful, but we insist on bringing in the clouds of our own doubt to dull this radiance. We are habituated to hiding our basic goodness and presenting those clouds of confusion, anxiety, jealousy, and aggression to the world instead.

There is a Tibetan term for the radiance of basic goodness: *ziji*. *Ziji* can be translated as "brilliant confidence" or "radiating splendor." It is the sense that when you let the clouds of your own confusion pass across the sky of your mind, the sun of basic goodness shines forth triumphantly. It is the natural manifestation of basic goodness: a confidence in your own ability to be a brilliant, kind individual. We can radiate that splendor to everyone we encounter, regardless of what we are wearing.

When you have faith in your own basic goodness, the brilliant confidence of *ziji* naturally arises. Chögyam Trungpa Rinpoche once said, "You may not have money to buy expensive clothes but . . . you can still express dignity and goodness. You may be wearing jeans and a T-shirt, but you can be a dignified person wearing a T-shirt and cut-off jeans. The problem arises when you don't have respect for yourself and therefore for your clothes."[4]

I recommend that you apply your mindfulness to how you dress. If you are present with the experience of picking out your clothes, donning them, making sure they fit and look right, that can be a mindfulness practice in and of itself. You are bringing your full self to the act of getting dressed. That can be an extraordinary experience. Even if you are in a T-shirt and jeans, you will look good because you are taking the time to connect with your innate dignity and goodness.

To invert this scenario, there are many people who spend lots of money on their clothes and look horrible. More often than not, they are so unattractive because they manifest their stuck emotions as opposed to their dignity. If you are angry and in a foul state of mind and you are completely disconnected from your basic goodness, then you can have a five-thousand-dollar dress on and it can't save you from looking like a jerk.

When I spent a brief stint as a monk, I learned from my teachers about how to take good care of my robes. They emphasized exactly how to put them on in the morning; it was a practice in and of itself for me. I was instructed to show great respect for these noble garbs. This is because our clothes can remind us about our inherent dignity and should not be considered something other than a vehicle with which to play out our mindfulness.

The more we meditate and tap into our heart and unearth our *ziji*, our confidence in our awake state, the more radiant we become. We are innately dignified. A good outfit can only aid us in expressing that dignity.

GETTING INK

Is it okay that I have tattoos?

Years ago I began contemplating getting a Buddhist symbol tattooed on my body. When one of my teachers, Kilung Rinpoche, came through town, I had the honor of hosting him at the meditation center I was running. While we were in private, I asked his opinion on whether it was disrespectful to the body to get a tattoo. "If it reminds you of something meaningful," he said, "then that is good. But that meaning can fade."

In other words, even if your tattoo continues to exist on your body for the remainder of this life, the meaning it carries for you personally may change and shift over time. Still, if you want to have significant reminders on your body, there is certainly nothing in the Buddhist canon that says you should not do that.

I myself do have a tattoo. It's not a Buddhist symbol; it is the initials of one of my best friends, who passed away much too young. For me it is a constant reminder of his love and his role in my heart. I am so inspired by his life that even glimpsing the tattoo on my arm while in the shower or when I wake up in the morning reminds me to live my life more fully. My heart becomes very tender every time I see his initials on my body. For me, at this time, it is a positive experience to have that tattoo. I am guessing that over time the feelings the tattoo inspires will morph and change, and I am open to that change as well.

That is the thing about tattoos—you think you are getting something fixed and permanent, but in fact it is subject to the same rules of change that the Buddha discussed twenty-six hundred years ago. The Buddha never gave specific instructions on tattoos, just as he did not give instructions to laypeople about how they ought to wear their facial hair or how often to bathe. He did, however, talk a good deal about a larger issue: nonattachment.

All phenomena change. This is not just something the Buddha said that we have to take his word for. We can all see that truth with our own eyes. You can walk around your childhood neighborhood and see that stores have closed down and then opened under different management, there are new neighbors that have moved in, everyone has gotten older, and you yourself have changed since you were a child. These are all very obvious things that can still be startling to us.

The fact of the matter is that we like to pretend that impermanence is not real. You might think that if you have a really great romantic relationship, for example, it will last your entire life. However, you and your partner are constantly changing individuals. It is as if you were dancing together, but as you both age and change, you may find yourself not as closely in step as you used to be. At some junctures of your life, you dance very intimately, and at others you find yourself drifting away from each other. You may break up or get divorced, or maybe one of you dies. This seemingly permanent aspect of your life can end quite abruptly. That is the nature of external circumstances. We are foolish to think otherwise.

The Buddha pointed out the reality of impermanence. As you read this, we are connected because both of us are getting older, both of our mental states are shifting, and our senses are taking in new sights and smells. Even though I am not in the room with you, you know this to be true. So in some sense, impermanence is a form of interdependence; we're all in this process of continuous change together.

The truth of change is particularly potent when we consider our bodies. The bodies of all of us morph moment by moment. If you adorn your body with something like a tattoo, that is fine and good, but you cannot expect that tattoo not to fade or its meaning not to shift over time. So it is best not to attach all of your happiness to that particular circumstance either.

I should point out that there will be some Buddhists out there who will disagree with me and claim that getting a tattoo is a horrible idea. That getting ink is disrespectful to your own body. That you are messing with something you ought to consider a sacred temple. With that image in mind, I would say to those people that I think that last notion is somewhat sound. The body *is* a temple, and we can honor that temple by adorning it with something of great meaning to us through having it imprinted on our bodies.

All of this said, I see no reason for it not to be okay to have tattoos and be a Buddhist. Just don't expect that tattoo to bring you long-term happiness or stay forever beautiful. The only type of beauty that is lasting is the inner glow we exude when we are fully connected to our own innate wisdom, that of our own basic goodness.

Facebook and Spare Time

If he was around today, would the Buddha have a Facebook page?

So much of Buddhism that's being applied to our modern world ends up coming back to your intention for engaging in a certain activity. Something like Facebook is not good or bad, but your intention can steer your actions in a virtuous or nonvirtuous manner. While I am not sure the Buddha would engage in Facebook himself, I do not think he would ever develop a "no Facebook" precept to rule anyone else out from doing so.

Many people have a mixed relationship with Facebook as well as other Web sites such as Twitter and Instagram. Some people think it is a giant waste of time, while others are delighted that they can learn so easily about friends who live far away. I myself use Facebook somewhat frequently, but I have never tried to convince myself that the time spent on the Web site is time spent cultivating mindfulness and compassion. It has proven helpful on occasion, as when, for example, I wanted to pick a large number of people's minds about what to call this book. A friend whom I have not seen in years suggested the existent title, which is a mini-Facebook success story in my mind. That is an occasion when I was able to use Facebook for something positive.

In its most basic form, though—for me and I'm guessing for others—Facebook is a distraction from the here and now. There is a slogan that has stayed relevant for years within the Shambhala Buddhist community that may apply: "Don't just do something, sit there." In other words, if you're engaging in Facebook, you're likely clicking over to the site just to "do something" as opposed to entering into that activity with any clear motivation.

If that is the case, then what you are doing is specifically taking time off from mindfulness. If you want to live a life based on mindfulness, then Facebook is likely not going to be used as a tool that will aid you in that endeavor. If you are spending more time on Facebook than, for example, meditating, then you are consciously saying that you would rather live a life based on distraction than on being present. We would live in a changed nation if everyone sat *shamatha* meditation for the same amount of time each day that they sat in front of their social-networking Web sites.

I have heard that at one point a student asked the Zen master Suzuki Roshi a question along these lines: "What should a Zen practitioner do with his spare time?" Suzuki Roshi reportedly looked perplexed. He began to repeat the phrase "spare time?" over and over again until he erupted into uproarious laughter. This idea that we have spare time, time that we can spend on things other than cultivating our mindfulness and compassion, was funny to him. We don't really have spare time; we only have time to dedicate to those endeavors as much as possible.

Sometimes a big change will be made to these social-networking Web sites and people will get upset. They feel that their privacy is being violated. When that happens, I often wonder what it is people are doing with their "spare time" that they are worried others will find out about. Some of us might use Facebook as a means to involve ourselves in negative emotions, giving them free reign while we envy our friend's vacation pictures or stalk an ex or silently judge the goings-on of others. I could be wrong here, but I believe that when people say they are worried about Facebook reporting their activity, there's an underlying tone of their not feeling good about the activity they are engaged in.

I am reminded of the old saying, "If you have nothing good to say, don't say anything at all." In this case, I believe we can apply that to how we spend our time on social-networking sites: if you don't want people judging your activity, don't engage in that activity. Obviously, this rule applies even after you power down your laptop, but it is particularly relevant when one click on your ex's wall can ruin your day as you discover she is dating again and another click can unfriend her, removing her from your newsfeed and maybe even from your life.

I can't imagine any enlightened being such as the Buddha sitting at his computer counting the number of friends he has or scrolling through all of the birthday wishes left on his electronic wall. It would shortchange him of the amount of time he has to spend in person with people he cares about or would like to be helpful to. Perhaps he would use the activity skillfully, having developed a set motivation to engage that medium for the purpose of sharing the dharma, maybe alerting people about where he would next be teaching.

For those of us who are not going to cut Facebook out of our lives, we need to be clear about why we visit it and what we want to get out of it personally and then keep sight of how that particular motivation fits in with the larger motivation for how we want to live our lives. I hope we can all learn to engage this site and others in a way that promotes mindful and positive behavior.

COMING OUT AS A BUDDHIST

How do I explain Buddhism to my religiously conservative parents?

I remember being in a bar one night when a newer meditator asked me about coming out to his parents as a Buddhist. "You make it sound as if you're telling them you're gay," I said. "Well, I think they would be more okay with that," he replied. "Being gay they understand. Buddhism, that's really weird to them."

If someone has never been exposed to meditation or Buddhist tenets, they can seem very weird and foreign. Whether you are talking with your religiously conservative family or a longtime friend who doesn't know much about what you're up to, you can apply basic Buddhist principles to help him or her understand what it is you do.

We have this training that can be applied to having these conversations. When you sit down to meditate, you become very inquisitive about your own self. You begin to poke and prod at this image you have of who you are, what your habits look like, whether they are helpful or harmful to you, and more. That is the process of getting to know yourself and befriending yourself.

When you are attempting to explain your understanding of Buddhism to people who are unfamiliar with it, you can apply this same level of inquisitiveness and curiosity. You can take a fresh-start approach to your family member or friend and treat the person with the same open-mindedness that you would if you had just met him or her for the first time. You apply the same open-mindedness that you offer yourself when you're on the meditation cushion. The more open and inquisitive you can be with another person, the more that person will want to reciprocate. This idea applies not just to friends and family but to people you want to date, work colleagues, really everyone you encounter.

In this case that may mean that you ask in-depth questions about what they know about Buddhism and investigate any preconceived notions they have about the religious tradition. As you engage your family member or friend, keep in touch with that fresh-start mind. Don't slip into "I knew she was going to say that" or "You would think that about meditation, wouldn't you." If you find that your parent or friend does not have a lot of knowledge about Buddhism, just be patient with the person.

At the same time, don't dumb down your experience of meditation or Buddhism. It's a tricky business, sharing your understanding of Buddhism without getting too complicated and losing someone or oversimplifying so the person walks away more confused than when you began. The simplest way to communicate your understanding effectively is to be fully present with the person with whom you are conversing.

Seung Sahn was once asked about a similar topic by a student who was trying to articulate basic Buddhist teachings. The Zen master said, "When you teach other people, just teach. Only teach; only help them. Don't worry whether or not they understand; only try. If you are trying 100 percent, then your teaching is complete and your mind-light will shine to them. Someday they will understand this."[5] You can follow Seung Sahn's advice by bringing your full self genuinely to this conversation.

Just offer what you experience, as opposed to your cerebral understanding. Don't fixate on whether you are saying the smartest or most articulate thing; just try and don't sweat it about whether the person understands every aspect of what you are saying. It is better that the person gets a hit of how meditation is affecting your presence than that she or he knows exactly what it is you do at your local meditation center.

Recently I was preparing for a rather large introductory meditation class. We had seventy people registered for the five-week course, which is double the size of an average class in this context. My coteacher and our teaching assistants seemed to be a bit nervous about accommodating everyone who was coming for the class. We talked a great deal about how to meet with everyone at least once individually and how we could encourage small-group discussions to facilitate a greater sense of community.

The staff and teaching assistants were expecting me and my coteacher to really deliver the goods when it came to offering inspiring talks that would keep people captivated and coming back week after week. "Look," I said after a bit, "whether people want to continue this course isn't going to come down to either of us giving a brilliant talk. It comes down to whether the students feel heard and accepted." I don't think that someone comes to understand Buddhism because he or she received all the right words in a talk and it made intellectual sense.

I believe the person wants to study the teachings further because he or she has a hit that someone is genuine in talking about how to relate to your own mind, and genuine is a rare commodity in today's world. With that in mind, when you sit down to talk to someone about your meditation practice or Buddhism on the whole, be genuine. Don't try to sound smart, but offer your experience and presence and see if the person can get an inkling of what you're working with.

Sometimes, particularly if you are talking to religiously conservative people, strong opinions of dissent arise. Seung Sahn had advice for this situation as well. He said, "You have your opinion. Your parents have their opinion. Your opinion and your parents' opinion are in conflict, so you have a problem. If you make your opinion disappear, then there will be no problem."[6] He actually offered this advice when someone asked him about how to manage parents' expectations around a wedding, but the teaching here still seems very relevant. If you can drop your fixed opinions and listen to the other person, that person may be more touched by your presence than by your debate tactics. Drop your opinions and see if there actually is any problem.

When it comes down to having this sort of conversation with one's parents, it is no easy task. The Buddha himself couldn't explain to his father why he wanted to pursue a spiritual life. He ended up having to flee in the middle of the night and pursue it wholeheartedly for years before contacting his father again. Only after he attained a true understanding of what he was doing, in this case attaining enlightenment, could he return to his family and offer his presence and explanations.

You don't have to wait until you are enlightened to talk to your parents about meditation. You can feel out their questions, really being inquisitive about their understanding of Buddhism. Then you can offer them your experience as opposed to your cerebral understanding. Don't try to get everything "right" in having this conversation but allow your presence to speak for you. Drop your set opinions around what they should take away from that conversation or how you would like it to run. Just be with whomever you are talking to, and your authentic presence will speak for itself.

MEDITATING AT THE STRIP CLUB

I know that in some meditation traditions people go to really rough places and meditate there. It's said that if you can meditate even when distracted, you are well trained. Is there anything like that in Tibetan Buddhism? Do you think we should do that more? Such as in intense work meetings? Or in seedy bars?

Within the Tibetan Buddhist tradition there are historically "rough places" where meditation practitioners can sit for extended periods of time and have the experience inform their practice. These rough places are known as charnel grounds. It is very hard to dig deep graves in the mountains of Tibet because of its incredibly cold climate, so people take their dead loved ones to these charnel grounds and leave the bodies there to decompose naturally aboveground.

Buddhist practitioners will go to these charnel grounds and meditate on the truth of impermanence and death. It is one thing to think that you will someday die. It's another to sit in front of a decomposing corpse as birds of prey peck at its skin. Going to a charnel ground is like staring death in the face; you have a more experiential understanding of this truth than if you sat in the comfort of your own home and thought a great deal about how everyone dies at some point. Pema Chödrön has said about charnel grounds, "It's in just such a place, surrounded by vivid reminders of death and impermanence, that brave meditators can practice staying awake and present under the most difficult circumstances. It's right there in the midst of such intensity that we can train most deeply in keeping the commitment to embrace the world."[7]

The Tibetan Buddhist teacher Khenpo Tsultrim Gyamtso Rinpoche talks a great deal about going to the places that scare you to train in preparation for death. Since we do not have areas intended for our meditation where we can go to watch dead bodies decompose, we have to come up with Western formats for charnel grounds. His suggestion, interestingly enough, is Disney World. You can ride a roller coaster, for example, and as you do you might freak out from the speed and intensity and think "I can really die here." In that case, the reality of death makes itself known. He instructs his advanced students to go on these rides and practice certain meditation techniques that they should end up doing at the time of death. In that sense, Disney World is the best meditation center on earth.

For many of us, it does not make sense to go to Disney World on a regular basis. It is expensive, and the lines are very long. Instead, you can determine for yourself a place where you can go out and meditate as a way to challenge your preconceived notions of the world and your practice. It could very well be an intense business meeting or a bar or even a strip club. These places may sound odd, but wherever we go, we can look to our surroundings as an environment where the truths of change and impermanence can and will play out.

If you are in a meeting and everyone is getting very speedy, shooting off ideas without much thought behind them, you can take that as an opportunity to cut through speed and aggression in your life. You can sit up straight, connect with your meditation posture, and focus on the breath. You don't have to make a big scene out of this simple meditation, but it is an excellent chance to see speed and not buy in to it. It is a bit like wading into a rushing river and planting your feet firmly on the earth. You experience the pull of the water but remain unswayed by it. As you then see speed in other aspects of your life—on your commute, when you are running late or out shopping—you can remember that you have already practiced cutting through this feeling of nonsense momentum and come back to the present moment. You are training in planting your feet and remaining present in the charnel ground known as work meetings.

Similarly, you can go to a seedy bar and treat that as your charnel ground. I was once asked by someone who was a biker whether she could be a Buddhist and still associate with her boyfriend, who was in a motorcycle club that participated in violent and sometimes illegal acts. At this point you may not be surprised that I encouraged my new friend to lean in and spend time with her boyfriend and his friends and, while not participating in any illicit activities, see if her openhearted presence might have a positive effect on any of them.

There is a word for this wholehearted aspect of our innate goodness, which is bodhicitta. This is a Sanskrit term that can be directly translated as either "open mind" or "awake heart." It is the idea that at a certain point our aim should not just be to try to avoid causing harm but to encompass everyone and everything we encounter as part of our spiritual journey. Every situation becomes a ripe opportunity for us to open our heart to reality as it is. It is easy to say that you want to practice *bodhicitta* and have an open heart with whomever presents him- or herself in your life. You might surround yourself with friends and family, people with whom it is easy to be openhearted. But that is not an intense training in *bodhicitta*. It is when your jerk of a boss barges into your office and yells at you for something that you did not do that you need to remember *bodhicitta*. It is when your biker buddies make an offhand remark about causing trouble that you can counter with something positive and kind. These are the times when you can best practice carrying an open heart, when you are faced with your habitual desire to close it down.

Similarly, if you want to cultivate *bodhicitta*, you can go to the areas that scare you, that threaten your ability to remain open, and be fully present with your heart in those circumstances. For my friend who was a biker, that meant her witnessing activities that she did not deem wholesome. Over time she found that she improved in offering her *bodhicitta* to these motorcycle club members and that they were willing to be open with her in kind. I don't know if anyone stopped committing violent acts because of her, but she was able to soften these very tough dudes just by offering her heart to them.

If you want to practice *bodhicitta*, you can certainly go to a seedy bar and remain openhearted regardless of what comes your way. You may have some people approach you and be friendly, or some drunk person may spill her or his drink on you or try to cause a fight. See if you can maintain your bodhicitta in both cases.

When I was younger my friends had a period of time where they would go to the occasional strip club. We were eighteen, and that seemed like a pretty cool thing to do now that we were legally allowed to do it. I had just started getting serious about meditation and came up with a wild notion: I would treat these clubs as charnel grounds and thus ripe grounds for practice.

While there were no decomposing corpses to remind me of death, I could instead witness the interplay of dancers and customers, complete with an opportunity to practice while seeing intense *shenpa,* or attachment. From my perspective, I thought the exotic dancers were attached to their desire for money and the customers were attached to their lust for the women dancing. Some of the female dancers were suffering from drug addiction, while some male customers felt so much apathy about their own partner that they didn't want to go home to her. No matter where you looked, fixed mind would present itself in that setting.

I held the view that strip clubs were charnel grounds for

many years. It was only last year, when I was on a book tour stop in Portland, Oregon, that I came to think differently about them. I met Caitlin and her boyfriend, John, at a bookstore reading. They were friends with the woman hosting me, and we all went out for drinks after the event.

After the initial period of getting to know one another, I asked Caitlin what she did for a living. "I'm a professional distraction," she said. I thought that was an interesting term and couldn't figure out if she worked in television, magazines, or what. There are so many distractions out there, and many of them need paid professionals to develop and promote them. "In other words," she finally said, "I'm an exotic dancer."

I was surprised, to say the least. Here Caitlin was a seemingly nice, balanced, Buddhist practitioner, and yet she was a stripper. She is also an artist and a writer, but her primary source of income comes from a strip club. As I continued to inquire about what that meant for her, she revealed that she doesn't drink or do drugs, nor does she engage her clients in any sort of sexual activity beyond a lap dance. She described herself as a performer, first and foremost, and the strip club as just another place she performs.

Meeting Caitlin transformed my fixed notion of what takes places at a strip club, and I found a kindred spirit in someone who was also practicing (albeit in a different format) bringing meditation off the cushion and into the strip club. Her practice was to treat everyone she encountered at work with deep respect and offer her *bodhicitta* to all of them. Whether she viewed the strip club as a charnel ground or a performance space or both was unclear, but she was less stuck on what the environment should be called and more interested in how she could embody her meditation practice in this place that is known for its suffering.

Imagine walking deep into a dark cave. It is easy for anyone to get lost in there. Many people are, in fact, stumbling around and tripping over one another in confusion. The good news is that you brought a flashlight with you. You turn it on, and all of a sudden everything in that deep, dark cave is illuminated. Everyone can see, and the people stop being so confused. That flashlight is your *bodhicitta*. It is the work of a true bodhisattva to go into the darkest aspects of our society in the hopes that he or she can serve as a light for all to see by.

The founder of the Kagyu lineage of Tibetan Buddhism, Tilopa, was just such a person. After Tilopa had gone deep with his own practice, one of his teachers instructed him to leave his regular meditation training and instead take two jobs. By day he would pound sesame seeds into oil. At night he would serve as the escort for men who wanted to sleep with the escort Dharima. In other words, he became a pimp.

While living among the prostitutes, Tilopa encountered a lot of pained, hardened hearts. He offered the prostitutes compassion and love, and over time they assimilated these characteristics of the meditation master. He softened them merely through his presence, and they were ultimately able to practice compassion themselves. It is through his time of pounding sesame seeds and serving as a pimp that Tilopa was able to attain true awakening and then be of most benefit to all beings.

In the same vein, we can take any of the rough spots of our society and treat them as excellent training grounds for mindfulness and compassion. Be it a boardroom, a bar, a biker gang, or even a strip club, you can enter into that situation with the view that you will apply your meditation practice to the act of being fully there and being of service to others. If you can maintain faith in your basic goodness, you can enter any scenario and be of aid to society, transforming yourself and others through your presence and *bodhicitta*.

3 / GETTING IT ON LIKE A BUDDHA

I was surprised that when *The Buddha Walks into a Bar* came out, people didn't want to talk to me about the bar. They wanted to talk about the bedroom. They wanted to talk about dating and long-term relationships and sex. Oh, did they ever want to talk about sex. I remember flying into Seattle and going to do an event at a meditation center there. After a few introductory remarks I asked what people wanted to talk about.

A woman in her fifties raised her hand. "I'm recently divorced," she started, "and I've been dating again." I thought I knew approximately where we might be going with this one. "The thing is, when I'm having sex with a guy and he comes and I'm not done, it's not always a big deal for me. Sometimes I just enjoy the act of having sex. But then he feels like less of a man because he didn't make me come. Then I no longer enjoy it because I have to soothe his ego by convincing him that it was good for me. What do you have to say about that?"

My friends like to joke that this is the only time they have ever seen me speechless. I think we talked about fixed expectations and how they can drag us down, how to communicate from the heart, and more, but then again, my mind was so blown away I'm not sure exactly how that conversation went down. I know the group in attendance that night had much more insight on this one than I did.

The thing is, I felt a lot of joy coming out of that event. I'm pretty sure that sort of issue had not been addressed within the hallowed walls of the meditation center, but this person was clearly a practicing Buddhist and was trying to apply her practice to her situation. Why shouldn't we talk about sex, dating, and love? These are valid aspects of our existence, so let us bring our practice to them.

LONELINESS, BEING SINGLE, AND YETIS

I've been single for a long time. Like, a really long time. I'm beginning to believe single, straight men are actually Yetis. I'm having trouble meeting people worth dating. Is it okay to be a Buddhist and go out to a bar or a club and try to pick someone up? I also feel that, as a Buddhist, I should just be happy with "right now." No matter how content I feel with the rest of my life, this loneliness is pervasive in my meditation, in my thoughts, in every moment.

Loneliness is something we have all felt at one point or time. When it hits, it hits hard and can feel all-pervasive. It could be sparked by yearning to meet a mate, by feeling homesick, by missing someone we love, or by just not feeling included. No matter what, it's a bitch.

You can approach loneliness the way you might try to approach other strong emotions: with kindness and curiosity. You can apply your meditative mind to this malady and really examine it thoroughly. Likely you have learned from past experience that beating yourself up over being stuck in emotional pitfalls is just draining energetically. As an alternative, you can explore your emotional states with a sense of gentleness and discernment. As my friend and Shambhala teacher Susan Piver once wrote, "Gentleness is the spiritual and emotional warrior's most powerful weapon."[1] Apply that weapon to your emotional state and see what happens.

If you are working with an emotion such as loneliness, one way to wield that weapon is to engage in a simple contemplation practice. Try taking your meditation posture and practicing *shamatha* for a few minutes. Once you feel grounded in your practice, see if you experience loneliness right now. If it is as pervasive for you as it is for the person who asked the question, it should come right up.

When you begin to experience loneliness, first be gentle with yourself. Ask yourself whether you can stay with this feeling or if it is too painful. If it is truly too painful, there is no shame in getting off the meditation cushion and instead going for a run or taking a shower, utilizing another healthy activity to aid you in calming down to the point that you can return to your meditation practice.

Assuming you can sit with your emotion, you can get inquisitive. You can ask yourself, "Where does loneliness reside in my body?" Sit with that question for a moment before asking yourself, "Does it have a shape? A color? Where does this emotion exist?" Then ask yourself, "Where did it come from?" Look for your emotion and see if it is as solid and real as you believe it to be. Conclude your session by relaxing your mind and resting in the present moment. When you are able, return to following the breath, return to *shamatha*.

Beginning to examine loneliness in this way frees you up from becoming too solid with your emotions. You begin to see that the emotion of loneliness is not as real and permanent as you may originally have guessed. That is liberation.

Emotions such as loneliness are transitional, like the clouds rolling across the sky. The clouds do not take on strong form and reside in the same place forever. They morph and change and gradually move along across the vast sky. While it may seem that emotions are heavier than clouds, if we examine them we realize they are just as fluid. "Right now," as our question asker noted, can be a source of happiness. Right now is as vast as the sky itself; reconnecting to it through meditation practice can be a powerful experience.

I found that two aspects of this question really held my mind—the idea that this person was having trouble finding someone "worth dating" and the notion that bars and clubs might not be a good place to find someone to date. Last year I began a series of workshops on bringing mindfulness into the dating world. It was based on the idea that we should be able to present our most authentic selves when we enter into a romantic encounter.

The workshop is entitled Slow Dating. It is a play on a recent phenomenon: the slow-food movement. Because fast food has become so prevalent, starting in 1986 a number of people have joined in the idea that we can counter the unhealthy aspects of those fast-food restaurants by preserving traditional cuisine based on local farming methods.

My idea was to counter the speed-dating culture that has popped up in Generation Y. Within speed dating you are given a very limited amount of time to sit down with a number of people and find out if you want to go on a date together. Friends who have gone to this sort of event have told me that they often felt flustered, that there wasn't a lot of time to connect with the other person, and that they spent their time trying to sell themselves, presenting only the most attractive aspects of who they are.

Slow dating is counter to that speed and the attempt to show off. It is based on meditation practice, where you are physically and mentally slowing down and connecting to your basic goodness. The workshop begins with contemplating the reason you are looking for someone to date. Is it because you are lonely and desire companionship? Is it because you are trying to get over a broken heart? Is it because you genuinely want to connect with someone? As with all things, knowing why we want to engage in an activity helps us clarify how we approach it.

The view of basic goodness is that when you are slowed down, you see yourself fully and can present all of yourself, as opposed to trying to offer your credentials as reasons someone should be attracted to you. It is not sitting down next to someone and telling the person all about your important job or listing all of the exotic vacations you have taken. It is touching your basic goodness and acting from that perspective.

When we are connected with basic goodness, a shift in view takes place. We begin to want just to be there with another person and experience that person for who he or she is, as opposed to projecting what we want from the person. At one point Pema Chödrön offered a very simple meditation instruction to a group of students: be fully present; feel your heart; and engage the next moment without an agenda. That is the practice of slow dating.

When you are present, touch your heart, and engage another person without an agenda, you may find that you are making an offering of yourself as you are. You are radiating *ziji*, that confidence that comes from living with an open heart. You are also acknowledging the other person's splendor and dignity. You are able to listen and discover who the person is.

With that in mind, the view of basic goodness teaches us that everyone we encounter is "worthy" of our time and energy. When the person who asked the question for this section mentioned that she was having trouble finding someone "worth dating," I thought back to when the Sakyong began using the word *worthy* more frequently in his teachings on basic goodness. When you discover your own innate wisdom, you develop confidence that you can do anything. With the perspective of basic goodness, you are capable enough, good enough, and worthy enough for whatever the world throws at you.

The funny thing is that it is not just you and me who possess basic goodness. It is everyone. So, in that sense, everyone is worthy of our getting to know them. We can form a genuine connection with anyone we encounter, should we drop our agenda and fixed views around what we think we need in a date to be happy. We can use deep listening as a practice in which we are inquisitive about our own self and curious about others. We can bring ourselves fully to these simple conversations and transform small talk with a big view.

When you are able to approach dating in this way, you may find yourself meeting lots of people. People are attracted to someone who is genuinely who she or he is. *Ziji* is sexy. When you are relaxed and genuinely appreciative of the other person, that person will want to learn more about you as well. Of course, this advice is not just about dating—we can bring ourselves authentically to all aspects of our life, to all of our meetings and interactions. The more we are available, the more possibility we see in the world and the more magnetizing we are in all ways.

As for picking someone up at a bar or club, I feel compelled to tell you that I was with a woman for four years who, and I kid you not, picked me up at a bar by asking, "So, do you come here often?" It was a preposterously bold move and pierced my self-involved bubble to the extent that we quickly formed a genuine connection. I was moved to learn more about her, and over the rest of the evening we were openhearted and connected in a more authentic way than I had been with anyone I had previously dated. There was no agenda: just conversation. That said, I certainly believe you can meet someone at a bar or club—so long as you take the time to be present, feel your heart, and approach the encounter without an agenda.

If none of this helps, my friend Dilip is single and a doctor. He's quite a stud muffin too.

Is It Okay to Be Gay?

I'm trying to become a Buddhist, but I'm struggling because I'm gay. Is there any restriction to being gay and being a Buddhist? If there is, please tell me.

First and most straightforwardly, no. There are no restrictions on being gay and being Buddhist. If you are gay and want to practice Buddhism, please feel extremely welcome. Now let's get complicated and go into the matter in-depth.

When the historical Prince Siddhartha became the Buddha,

he taught extensively. Yet somehow, in the midst of all of his teachings, nothing shows up in the Pali cannon that explicitly comes down on homosexuality. It's as if he didn't even think to mention homosexuality, which is odd, considering it was present in India at the time. My interpretation here (and a number of other people have also written about this) is that since the Buddha did not make specific classifications in his teachings, we can infer that he meant to lay out the same rules for homosexual behavior that apply to heterosexual behavior.

So let's explore these rules, specifically the third of the five precepts: *kāmesu micchācāra veramaṇī sikkhāpadaṃ samādiyāmi*. This is the precept saying that one should abstain from sexual misconduct. The term *sexual misconduct* has been interpreted and reinterpreted countless times. My personal interpretation is that the Buddha set out to pursue a life of spiritual awakening that ended with the idea that, above all, we should do no harm to others or to ourselves. Yet any time you have sex with someone, you create a certain number of ramifications, some of which can include hurt feelings, disease, or awkward party run-ins. In other words, harm.

Some scholars have suggested that in a strict interpretation we would all need to remain celibate in order to ensure that no one gets hurt. Anything other than that would be sexual misconduct. But that would mean that if everyone became Buddhist and went by that rule, the human race would die out in a single generation.

Looser interpretations have implied that so long as you are not a monastic and you practice safe and consensual sex, you are keeping within the spirit of the precept. My sense of appropriate sexual conduct for heterosexuals and homosexuals alike tends toward the looser "have sex and try hard not to cause harm, and please use a condom" attitude. As with all of these topics, what is most important is your own understanding of how the traditional teachings apply to your life.

It's worth noting that some Buddhists disagree with the whole "what's good for heterosexuals is good for homosexuals" approach. A painful example to me in this regard is the Dalai Lama. Yes, he is a spokesperson for the Tibetan people and the reincarnation of the bodhisattva of compassion, but the guy really put his foot in his mouth at a press conference back in June 1997. He said, "From a Buddhist point of view [lesbian and gay sex] . . . is generally considered sexual misconduct."

To be fair, the Dalai Lama later clarified that he was quoting tradition on how oral sex, anal sex, and masturbation are considered taboo. The same text—by the fourteenth-century Buddhist teacher Tsongkhapa—that he was referencing also prohibits sexual intercourse during daylight hours. I am guessing that most of us have, at some point, broken at least one of these rules. This means it is not just homosexuals who are being condemned here but anyone who likes any form of spice in the bedroom or wants to see his or her partner in the light of day. Also, the texts His Holiness referenced imply that homosexual relationships are okay; it's just these sexual acts that are not.

I, for one, am not a fan of this monastic Tibetan Buddhist party line. I have great respect for meditation masters such as Tsongkhapa, Gampopa, and Dza Patrul Rinpoche who have written about these various prohibitions. However, these teachers were writing for a particular time and place. People are people, and I doubt that the Buddha would have wanted to prevent anyone from pursuing enlightenment because of her or his sexual orientation.

As we have been discussing thus far in this book, Buddhism has spread throughout the world, and as it has encountered new cultures it has continued to adapt to meet societal norms. This has led to some aspects of Buddhism's being interpreted strictly in one locale (fourteenth-century Tibet) and quite loosely in another (America today). Of course, Buddhism is not the only religious tradition that has such a range of interpretation on hot-button topics.

In conclusion, I know many, many Buddhists who are gay

and are wonderful meditation practitioners. The Buddha pursued a life that teaches us that we need to look at our actions and determine whether they are helpful, based on good intentions, and free from harm or if we are just being a douche bag. Qualities such as mindfulness and compassion can be practiced by all of us, regardless of sexual orientation, race, ethnic background, income, or what have you. So if you are gay, bisexual, or any other form of orientation, welcome to Buddhism; it's great to have you as a fellow practitioner on this path.

GETTING DOWN WITH YOURSELF

> Is masturbation allowed in Buddhism? Some medical articles state that it's harmless for health, but what does Buddhism say about this issue?

This question somewhat dovetails with the one about homosexuality in that we can look to the five precepts for monastics as a resource for what the Buddha might have recommended vis-à-vis pleasuring yourself. According to the third precept, the one involving sexual misconduct, if you are a monk or nun, you are not supposed to engage in any sexual conduct, including manual sex, that is, masturbation. In fact, there are all sorts of fun details that the monastic community adopted because some members of the sangha were fixated on trying to cling to the letter as opposed to the nature of the law. Supposedly some monks ended up doing things like walking through tall grass without wearing underwear with their robes as a way to skirt the masturbation issue (hey, whatever works, right?).

It does not make sense to cling to the letter of these laws. The Buddha himself said in the Kalama Sutra, "Rely not on the words of the teaching but on the spirit of the words. Rely not on theory but on experience." Let's talk about the experience of masturbating in today's world, as lay practitioners of Buddhism.

As nonmonastic practitioners we don't need to subscribe to the strict interpretation of the third precept. Based on the Buddha's words in the Kalama Sutra, we should not go the route of "this is what the monastic order decided to do twenty-six hundred years ago so we need to do things exactly that way now" but instead we can consider "am I causing harm to myself or others?" If pleasuring yourself is causing harm, don't do it. If it isn't, I don't see an issue here. Before engaging in an action such as regular masturbation, one way you can check on your own experience is to ask yourself, "Will I feel better or worse when this is over?"

Let me posit another idea: that sometimes pleasuring yourself can actually save you from causing harm. Let's imagine you are out on the town and meet a beautiful member of the sex you are attracted to. You flirt, you swap numbers, and then you part ways. I'd like to think that instead of getting horny or drunk and dialing up this person, the more appropriate way to cool down would be to take some "me" time. Granted, there are other alternatives to engaging in promiscuous behavior besides masturbating, but that may very well be the appropriate skillful means for you in that context.

To address the second part of this question, I want to point out that not only is masturbation deemed harmless to health, there are all sorts of studies that have deemed it beneficial for things like lowering your blood pressure, helping create harmony in relationships, lowering the chance of prostate cancer for men, and leaving you in a relaxed and contented state.

The Buddha did, however, say a lot about how we should neither be attached to nor crave sensual pleasure. Desire and lust are easy things to become attached to, and as we know, attachment causes us suffering. In other words, don't overdo it. If you see yourself choosing masturbation over work, time with friends, or your meditation practice, then that's a problem. That is one way you may be causing harm to yourself, by clinging to your attachment to pleasure. In talking about sexual acts, Chögyam Trungpa Rinpoche once said, "What is important is seeing the passion clearly."[2] So examine the passion behind the craving to masturbate.

Masturbation can also serve as a distraction or a means of avoidance of spiritual practice. Sure we could go sit on the cushion for a half hour, but thinking of naked writhing bodies sounds like more fun, right? Agreed. So while there are no hard-and-fast rules for lay practitioners on when or how to masturbate, I would say that you should not overindulge to the point where playing with yourself means less time for playing with the dharma.

Doing It . . . a Lot

I like to have sex with a lot of different people; sometimes I am more interested in the sex than the person. I think this may harm people.

I am reminded of a story about the Zen teacher Suzuki Roshi. Apparently, during a question-and-answer session, one of his students asked him about sex. The student admitted to having a lot of sexual desire and that he was thinking of becoming celibate as a means to address that longing. He asked for Suzuki Roshi's advice. Suzuki Roshi acknowledged the question and said, "Sex is like brushing your teeth. It's a good thing to do, but not so good to do it all day long."

When it comes to specific advice on sex, the view Suzuki Roshi presents is a good one to have. As lay practitioners, it is okay to engage in acts such as sex or masturbation, but don't make it your main activity or let it distract you from other aspects of your life that you care deeply about. It can be a good thing to do, but not if it is the only thing you do. Also, don't brush your teeth all day long, or your gums will bleed.

Looking at Suzuki Roshi's advice, we can see that there is nothing wrong per se with a lay practitioner having sex. Chögyam Trungpa Rinpoche agreed with this notion when he said, "There is a certain tendency to think that sex, unless you are married or in some other prescribed situation, is something naughty. . . . Such attitudes automatically undermine the sacredness of sexual communication."[3] Sex can be considered a sacred act. If you are giving fully of yourself to another human being, be it in conversation, through volunteer work, or in sex, that is a sacred act.

However, if you begin to suspect that your intention is to have sex for the sake of sex and you don't really care about the persons you are having sex with, you have a problem. Trungpa Rinpoche went on to say in the same lecture, "Once someone begins to regard the sexual act as a frivolous thing, the whole approach toward sex becomes very cheap. The attitude of people toward each other becomes frivolous as well, as though they were using each other purely as property."[4] In that case, you are not acknowledging your partner as a genuine human being, someone with her or his own open heart and confusion, but as a plaything. That is a view to be given up.

If you are more interested in the act of sex than in the person you are having sex with, then you are treating the person with very little respect. That is an unhealthy way to view anyone you are spending time with and particularly someone you are sleeping with. It is an attitude that can create a great deal of harm, both to you and to the other person, and you ought to discard it.

In general, if you think you are harming people, stop doing the activity that you think may be causing harm. It is always wise to err on the side of caution when it comes to risky behavior, be it making out with your friend's ex, getting drunk with colleagues, or having casual sex. Sakyong Mipham Rinpoche once acknowledged a habitual way we view the world when he said, "We look at people with the attitude of taking, not of giving."[5] He encouraged us to switch that perspective around so that we look at everyone we encounter as opportunities for giving of ourselves as opposed to resources we can suck from.

If your view in having a lot of sex is to connect with people and commit, even briefly, to having genuine experiences with them in a way that you both understand to be beneficial, awesome. You may very well be able to have a lot of sex and not cause harm. It's possible, sure. But it is hard to do.

The Dalai Lama is known to have said, "Our prime purpose in this life is to help others. And if you can't help them, at least don't hurt them." I think that advice is an excellent guide for taking on sexual activity with others. At the bare minimum, don't hurt your partners. You can communicate from the heart with the person you are having sex with, making sure that your intention meshes with his or her own, and continue to check in on how you are both feeling. Through speaking and listening from the heart, you are less likely to cause harm to that individual. Ideally, you are helping the person through the act of being intimate with him or her. But really, don't cause harm in the name of getting off. Just don't do it.

DROPPING EXPECTATIONS ON MATCH.COM

I realize the Buddha didn't have the Internet in his lifetime. I've been contemplating joining an online dating Web site but am not sure if it's the best thing to do. Is there anything non-Buddhist about finding a partner online?

With so many people out there looking to meet other singles, it's no surprise that online dating has become a big trend. From a conventional point of view, it has gotten easier to meet someone these days; you don't even have to leave your own home. For people who are averse to meeting someone at a bar or parties or are a bit shy or are new to an area, this seems like a good option.

I don't see anything "non-Buddhist" about finding a partner online. There are some aspects of that process that might make it more complicated than meeting a partner in person, specifically around presenting yourself authentically and dropping fixed expectations of your potential mate.

If you are going to do online dating and want to apply Buddhist principles to that act, start by presenting yourself authentically. When you go onto one of these dating Web sites, you are asked a number of questions about yourself. It is tempting to present only the best aspects of yourself—and even exaggerate them a little. You might add an inch to your actual height or shave a year or two off your actual age or make your job sound more impressive than it is in real life.

I would recommend trying to avoid anything other than being straightforward on a dating site. The process of meditation enables us to become familiar with and acknowledge that we are basically good as we are. We can present that to others without fear. The view of basic goodness is that regardless of who the other person may be, we are worthy enough of that person's love.

I am reminded of a story about my friend Ivan. He himself had a friend who had met someone on Match.com and asked Ivan's advice about whether he should go on a date with her. Ivan had trouble trying to look at her profile online, so he had to create an account of his own to do so. Early on in that process he was asked to give himself a username. Thinking he would never return to the site, he typed in "NotSoWellHung." He logged on to the site, gave his friend the thumbs up, and moved on with his life.

The funny thing is that he started getting e-mails. Woman after woman would write to him and say how funny his username was and how much they appreciated that he wasn't trying to puff himself up but was willing to throw it all out there, and would he by any chance be interested in having a drink together. After a period of time, he had to shut down his account on the Web site so that his inbox would not be flooded by women enamored with his openness. While I always love teasing Ivan about this story, it does illustrate that people are indeed attracted to authenticity, even on dating Web sites.

Not to kick a dead horse on this front, but assuming you do end up meeting someone on a dating Web site, your small fibs may quickly catch up with you. If you haven't presented yourself authentically, the really small stuff might be highlighted early on. You said you were one weight, but really you packed on some pounds around the holiday. Your picture looked flawless, but you can't hide that blemish that appeared on your forehead this week. You said you were five eight, but you're really five six, and since your date is five six, that is apparent pretty quickly. If you do not present yourself authentically online, then you may end up apologizing for yourself before you even get to know your potential mate.

Let's say, though, that you do present yourself genuinely on a dating Web site. The other main obstacle you might want to look out for is falling into fixed expectations. Let's say you are on Match.com and you see someone you think is cute. Bonus: this person also likes puzzles and Judd Apatow comedies. You will have a lot to talk about. You begin to fantasize about what your first date would look like, what you would talk about, the laughs you would share quoting your favorite movies. You could date for a few months, then move into his place because you live with roommates, and then after living together for a year, maybe he would ask you to marry him—by way of a puzzle spelling out the proposal.

It's important to remember that the person listed on a dating Web site is not a complete person but a résumé of sorts. It is listed information that the person is presenting in the hopes that others will be attracted to him or her. If you limit your understanding of that person to what you read or to a few messages you pass back and forth, you will have very set expectations regarding who the person is when you do actually meet. If you walk into a meeting with someone thinking you already know her or him, then your relationship is doomed from the start.

When we set expectations for our partner in any scenario, it spells trouble. If we do so without having ever met the person face-to-face, then it seems like a recipe for disaster. A romance fueled by wishful thinking and set expectations is not going to be a lasting one.

I think anyone who wants to try online dating should go ahead and give it a chance. But be authentic about who you are as much as you can, given the format. Try not to fixate on trying to find an ideal partner who shares all of your interests. Drop your fixed expectations of what you need to be happy and just experience people for who they are. When we do that, we enjoy true happiness, no matter the outcome of our meeting. Last but not least, make sure that when you open up your membership you also keep an open mind.

Open Relationships

What is the Buddhist take on open relationships? Can we have multiple partners at once and still be Buddhist?

The other night I was discussing this topic of open relationships with a friend, and he referred to Buddhism as something of an "anything goes" religious tradition. I don't think that's necessarily true, but to invert that idea, maybe it's something like an "a lot of things aren't necessarily restricted, assuming you are using the activity as a means to become awake" religious tradition. Somehow I don't think that slogan will catch on as quickly, but it feels more accurate.

I know many Buddhists who do indeed date around quite a bit, as well as some who are in open relationships with their spouse. Neither of these things has ever really worked out for me, but I can't fault other people for doing this, assuming their intention is to reduce harm and benefit others. I can't imagine anyone finding out about my friends' relationship status and all of a sudden barring them from the local meditation center; they are just as valid Buddhists as anyone else I know. The simple answer here is yes: it is possible to have multiple partners and still practice Buddhism.

In terms of our historical friend Sid, it's purported that he himself did have multiple partners. At one point the Zen teacher and author Brad Warner referred to Siddhartha as "the Gene Simmons of the spiritual scene," referring to the idea that he got around. However, it's worth making a clear distinction here between Palace Sid and Seeking Enlightenment Sid.

Palace Sid was a guy who lived in a palace. He lived a sheltered existence, where his father made sure he was constantly surrounded by lots of distractions to ensure that he would never have to think of life beyond the palace walls or know suffering of any kind—and certainly not live a life devoted to the spiritual benefit of others. That ultimately fell apart when the Buddha asked to see the world beyond his palace and caught glimpses of the pains we all endure: sickness, old age, and death. He also saw a spiritual practitioner and thought, "Huh. I could do that."

Palace Sid morphed into Seeking Enlightenment Sid after that. Seeking Enlightenment Sid realized that suffering existed in a very real way. His jaw dropped, and he realized he had to do something about all of this pain, so he left the palace, went out into the world, and pursued meditation practice wholeheartedly.

Interestingly enough, that is exactly what Sid discovered when he sat down to meditate: his whole heart. As he attained nirvana, his mind and heart opened in a vast and fathomless manner, such that he was able to perceive reality as it is. The more we become familiar with our own suffering, the more we begin to see how other people suffer too. If you are sitting on the meditation cushion and you feel bombarded by jealous thoughts, that is a time for you to cut through this habitual thinking and come back to the present moment, come back to the breath. The more you come back to the present, the more you are loosening the hold jealousy has on you.

When you are going about the rest of your life, you will notice when jealousy rears its ugly head and will, ideally, come back to the present moment instead of giving in to that story line. The more you evade that hook of jealousy, the more available you are to the rest of your world. You are present to what is going on around you, and it breaks your heart in the best way possible.

Previously, you may have thought that you were the only one being hooked by jealousy. It was something that you and only you struggled with on a daily basis. However, your coworker is being particularly snide to you since you were promoted. Your sister seems annoyed by the amount of attention your parents have been showering on you. Your friend says he never sees you anymore since you started dating someone new. You are not perplexed by these reactions: you are awake enough to realize that these individuals have been snagged by jealousy too.

When you see in yourself this emotion that you thought you had evaded, you do not get defensive. Instead, there is the birth of compassion. You know jealousy well. You might say, "Ah, jealousy, my old friend. It's been days since I've seen you. Come and have some tea with me." You invite this emotion back into your life because you have been practicing looking at it without letting it get its hooks into you.

You see that your coworker and sibling and friend carry this incredible burden of jealousy, and you long for them to be rid of their strife. You know how painful it is to be hooked by jealousy, and so you lean in and communicate with them, offering your open heart and mind, such that they might learn to be free of this afflictive emotion. Pema Chödrön recognized the pain of these strong emotions and said, "There's no way to make a dreadful situation pretty. But we can use the pain of it to recognize our sameness with other people."[6] Compassion is based on realizing that while story lines may change, we all suffer in the same way.

The example of jealousy is relevant to our discussion about the birth of compassion. If you are in an open relationship, jealousy may be forever knocking at your door. You may end up hooked by jealousy when your partner goes home with someone new, or your partner may end up jealous when you go out on a first date with someone else. To know emotions like jealousy is to see through emotions like jealousy. It is the cleanest way not to let the emotion get its hooks in you. It is the most efficient way to have compassion for other people who do get hooked by their emotions.

Chögyam Trungpa Rinpoche said, "Compassion is also communication, the ultimate communication."[7] In this sense, when you give birth to compassion, you can take on a form of skillful means: communication. You can lean in and explore whatever suffering exists within your open relationship or any relationship you have in your life, be it with friends, family, or lovers. When you do, you can communicate with the view of *bodhicitta*, an open heart that can accommodate everything. You can explore with your partners whether you share the same intention for being together, if they have the same values as you do, and if you can enter into a relationship with the idea that you will continue to change, be open to one another, and serve one another genuinely and fearlessly. If you can base your relationship in *bodhicitta* and compassion, then it is a true Buddhist partnership.

YOU ARE WORTHY OF LOVE

I have difficulty seeing myself as worthy of love. I doubt I'll ever find a partner. I feel alone and unlovable.

Over the last few years I have seen variations on this topic of worthiness appear frequently. Often I see some version of this question at the end of a long meditation workshop. To close out these programs, each participant has the opportunity to offer anonymously an issue that he or she is working with in his or her own life. Given the cloak of anonymity, people feel free enough to strike at this core feeling of despair.

We would be sitting in a circle and I would pull a piece of paper out of the bowl, and my heart would immediately break upon reading the topic to be discussed. Sometimes this question was phrased as someone feeling that her partner did not actually love her and she didn't have confidence in her ability to be loved. Other times it was based on feeling alone. More often than not, the person asking the question says he feels that he is not worthy of another person's love.

We live in a society that is based on highlighting our short-comings. The makeup ads, the perfectly manicured celebrities, the thousand-dollar suits and dresses that adorn them, every-thing highlights just how not put together enough we are. We have society yelling in our ear, saying, "Everyone has their act together except you. I swear!" Of course, that is simply not the case. Everyone, including the fantastical celebrities, has issues. I can't imagine that the latest twenty-something movie star go-ing through her second divorce doesn't worry that she is inher-ently unlovable.

The view of basic goodness is that we are already per-fect. We are already amazing, just as we are. We are eminently lovable. If you can learn to develop faith in that notion, then you will realize your own self-worth. It is so important to develop faith in basic goodness. Pema Chödrön says, "I can't overestimate the importance of accepting ourselves exactly as we are right now, not as we wish we were or think we ought to be."[8]

I recommend a simple contemplation practice for when-ever you are plagued by doubts of your inherent worth. If you find yourself lost in poverty mentality, thinking you are not good enough for true love or your position at work or to handle a crisis in your family life, just pause. Drop all story lines around your doubt and just experience it for what it is: another ephemeral emotional state. Regardless of whether you are on the meditation cushion, on the subway, or in a meeting, you should just tune in to your environment. Notice the sights, sounds, smells around you.

Then bring your full attention to the phrase "At my core, I am basically good." See what responses arise as you try to hold your mind to that simple phrase. Don't judge your reactions, just let them rise up and fall away again. After a minute or two of that contemplation, bring your mind to the phrase "I am worthy of this moment." Notice what responses come up, but keep bringing your mind back to this phrase. After another few minutes, turn your mind to one final phrase: "I have everything I need." Having spent perhaps five complete minutes with these three phrases, raise your gaze to the horizon and drop all thoughts. Don't contemplate or meditate on the breath. Just be with what is going on in that moment.

In any moment we have a choice. We can give in to society's exhortations to be despondent because we will never be good enough to succeed in love, work, or family. Or we can listen to our own basic goodness, allowing that intuitive voice to guide us toward awakening to our full potential. We can hear that voice urging us to realize that we can accept ourselves exactly as we are, that we are already complete.

When we listen to the societal whisper of doubt regarding our own goodness, we end up feeling alone and unlovable. When your relationship has broken up or you have been single for a long time, you might begin to doubt that you will ever again find someone who loves you for yourself. Particularly as you start to get a bit older and you see all of your friends pair off and get married, you may feel that you have missed the boat and will end up alone, with cats, until you die—and will then not be found for weeks, the cats having gotten hungry and eaten you.

That is an extreme form of doubt. It is based on the idea that you are not okay. You are not good enough to be loved or to be worthy of another person's admiration, so you will live a miserable life because no one will care for you in any way. It assumes that true happiness is to be found in external circumstances, in this case a partner who will always be around and supportive and will not die before you.

When you are hooked by this trap of doubt, you can remind yourself of two things:

1. Everything Is Impermanent

My father's dentist used to joke that there can't be a hell because you can get used to anything in three days. I like that idea, particularly coming from a dentist, someone whose profession may end up causing a bit of pain here and there. The notion behind impermanence is that it's not just good stuff that changes, morphs, and fades away. It's not just our romantic partners or family members or friends that move, die, or part ways with us. It is the bad stuff too. It is the heartbreak when you are dumped and the grief when someone dies and the feelings of inadequacy that move across your life like a tumbleweed in an old Western movie. Even if you try to solidify pain and cling to it, it ends up evolving over time such that you move beyond it.

Thus, even feelings such as loneliness and the idea that you are unlovable will change eventually. You will spend time with good friends whose company you enjoy, or you will find a mate who appreciates you and your eccentricities, or you will get used to being alone and find contentment within that basic experience. Everything is impermanent, so there is actually very little to worry about in this lifetime.

2. Basic Goodness Never Fades Away

The one thing that will not fade or go away is our innate wakefulness. In traditional texts it is referred to as primordial, in that it has no beginning and no end. Our ability to wake up is always available to us, like a well that has unlimited water rushing into it. No matter how much we drink of our wakefulness, there is always more of it to enjoy.

If you can overcome your doubt, you can connect with the view of basic goodness. You can soak in the cool, refreshing waters of this fathomless well of awake. Even if society whispers in your ear that you are unlovable or that you will end up with one hundred cats, you can take a sip of your own goodness and acknowledge that those whispers are ephemeral and they too shall pass.

FIDELITY AND HONESTY

> My best friend is cheating on his girlfriend with a woman he met on a work trip. He's confided it to me, and I hate it—having to bear the burden of knowing this, when his girlfriend is a good person who doesn't deserve to be treated this way. I haven't yet told him that I disapprove, which I will, but I can't decide whether to tell his girlfriend, as I think she should know. On one hand, I want to respect the confidence he's shown in me by sharing this, and on the other hand, I don't want her to be hurt, and I could probably handle losing his friendship. But it's all so complicated. What the hell would the Buddha do in a case like this?

Any time you are stuck between two people you are in a hard situation, but a situation like this one is particularly tricky. At the end of the day, when you face difficult situations, you want to feel good about how you handled them. You want to feel that you reduced suffering for yourself and others. It is hard to discern how to do that at times. But leaning in with this aspiration and exploring each difficult scenario you encounter in your life seems like a good way to start addressing the challenge.

Previously I mentioned how straightforward communication can be seen as a form of compassion. Compassion takes many forms. Sometimes it is gentle, where you are supportive of someone who is down on his or her luck and offer the person resources such as a shoulder to cry on or a home to stay in. Other times compassion may look a bit more wrathful.

When you visit a Tibetan Buddhist community, you may see *thangkas*, traditional paintings that depict deities, scenes, or iconography. There are many that display wrathful beings of compassion. One traditional deity I have always felt drawn to within Shambhala is the Four-Armed Mahakala. *Mahakala* is a Sanskrit word that can be translated as "great black one."

Mahakala is a fierce and powerful demon that is said to have been brought to serve the dharma by the fourth Trungpa Tulku. He bound the Four-Armed Mahakala as a protector of his monastery, Surmang, where the being has protected the holy teachings of the Buddha ever since. The great eleventh-century Buddhist teacher Machik Labdrön once said, "In other traditions demons are expelled externally. But in my tradition demons are accepted with compassion."[9] So this demon was transformed through compassion and brought to the dharma. He is black in color and terrifying in face and has four arms; Mahakala looks like the last being you would think of as an example of compassion.

However, if you look closely, there is a lot of compassionate symbolism in the depiction of the Four-Armed Mahakala. One of his left arms holds a skull cup of *amrita,* which is the intoxicating nectar of the gods. This intoxicating *amrita* is a means of pacifying energy. One of his right arms holds a hooked knife, which is a symbol of enriching, extending positive influence and dignified qualities to others. The other right arm holds a sword, which is a way of magnetizing energy. The sword is not meant to be used as a weapon, but by waving it Mahakala is rallying and magnetizing resources. His other arm on the left side holds a trident, which symbolizes destructive energy. Each prong is meant to cut through passion, aggression, or ignorance, literally annihilating obstacles.

Within this image of the Four-Armed Mahakala we see four skillful ways that compassion can manifest: pacifying, enriching, magnetizing, and destroying. If you get into a fight with your spouse, you might want to consider pacifying the situation. "Look honey," you might say, "what if we talked about this tomorrow when we calm down? Let's sleep on it and see if this is a real issue in the morning." That is an example of pacifying compassion. If your friend is depressed, you may want to take her or him out somewhere fun, such as a museum, so that the friend can feel uplifted. That is enriching the person's situation, another form of compassion. If you are working with a colleague to start a business, you might go out and meet with potential advisors and investors, trying to magnetize resources such as experience and money to get your endeavor going. You are expressing compassion to your business and to your investors by magnetizing resources to something you all believe in.

Alternatively, you may have a friend who continues to go back to his abusive spouse. In that example, you sit down with him and try to highlight what a bad idea that has been in the past. While it may be painful for your friend to hear these words, if they come from seeing reality as it is rather than from your own fixed mind-set, then your words are destructive to his perspective but helpful to him long-term. That is compassion in the form of destruction.

Chögyam Trungpa Rinpoche was the reincarnation of the Trungpa Tulku who brought the Four-Armed Mahakala to the dharma. He once said, "The whole structure of the image is based on energy and complete compassion devoid of idiot compassion."[10] In other words, the image of Mahakala is unbiased, wholehearted compassion. Whichever of these four methods of compassion Mahakala needs to deploy, he is ready to deploy.

Within Trungpa Rinpoche's quote above there is a term he coined: *idiot compassion*. Idiot compassion is the idea, for example, that turning to your friend who keeps going back to his abusive ex and encouraging him to leap in and repeat the same cycle of suffering is not genuine compassion at all. It is enabling habitual behavior, which is perpetuating pain for all parties concerned. Idiot compassion is being nice to be nice as opposed to seeing a situation for what it is and acting in accordance with that reality. While it may be harder to do, speaking to your friend about why it may not be a good idea to leap toward abuse is true compassion.

Mahakala is supposed to guide and protect meditation practitioners from all kinds of deception and delusion. This includes the delusion we carry about what we think needs to happen and the deception that we find ourselves subject to when we care about others and they betray us.

To return to the question of fidelity, without knowing the individuals involved in this very elaborate cheating scenario, I cannot weigh in one way or another about what it is best to do. If you found yourself in this situation, the most compassionate thing might be to tell the girlfriend in a straightforward manner what you know, which is compassion based on destroying her idea of her honest relationship. It might include listening to her response, being there for her in a pacifying manner. Alternatively, it might be to turn to your friend and strongly encourage him to fess up, which is also destructive compassion, as it is based on popping his notion of getting away with his shit.

In general, it is wise to be as straightforward with your friends as you can, without being hurtful. You can tell your friend who is the cheater how uncomfortable you are holding this secret. You can encourage him to talk to his girlfriend and come clean. You can try to make him see that he has caused true harm not only to his partner but also to you by putting you in such an uncomfortable position. We can hope that your speaking straightforwardly from your heart will open his. If so, he comes clean to his girlfriend and you are in the clear. If not, it's hard to predict how the scenario will play out and what your role in it might be.

The historical Buddha never taught a sutra on what to do if your friend is cheating on his girlfriend. However, if you were to take the five precepts of monastic Buddhism as your guide, you would be under no real pressure to say or do anything without prompting. The most helpful thing in some cases is not to speak at all but to listen deeply. The fourth precept reads *musāvādā veramaṇī sikkhāpadaṃ samādiyāmi*. In English we can translate that as "I undertake the precept to abstain from false speech."

False speech can be interpreted in a number of different ways. In a strict interpretation, it could just be saying "don't lie." If your buddy's lady comes up and asks if your friend cheated, then you might feel obligated not to lie to cover for him. However, expositions of this precept often include other harmful speech, such as slandering others, gossiping, and abusing others with your speech. The way I have always thought of this precept is that if you are going to cause harm when you open your mouth, don't open it. This seems like a good rule not just for monastics but for everyone.

One important thing to consider before pulling the trigger and getting involved through any of the four methods of compassion as displayed by the Four-Armed Mahakala is whether you are creating lasting harm or are offering your point of view with the best of intentions and expect it to lead to good. Even temporary harm with a large side of good might prompt you to speak up. But in all cases, I recommend being straightforward.

BUDDHIST WEDDING ADVICE

I'm engaged! It's magical and exciting and romantic and all of those truly wonderful things. I'm sure you've officiated a wedding or two in your life—what are the most important words of wisdom you'd announce to the bride and groom for a happy, mindful life together? In other words, how would a Buddhist conduct a wedding ceremony?

Congratulations! I have indeed officiated at a few weddings in my short life. Any time two people come together to celebrate their love and commitment to each other, it is a beautiful thing. As I have mentioned before, one cannot say that marriage will bring everlasting happiness, as all external circumstances are subject to change, but a wedding is a particularly potent time to celebrate and appreciate the love we do share with someone in this very moment. In fact, acknowledging impermanence and change only heightens the notion that two people should cherish the time they have together.

The most important words of wisdom I generally impart to couples committing to spending their lives together is to continue to take a fresh-start approach to their partner, day after day, year after year. In the beginning of a relationship, we have a natural curiosity about the person we are spending all of our time with and want to know all of the beloved's little quirks and eccentricities.

Unfortunately, as time wears on, many of us think we know our partner. We stop being inquisitive about him or her, and as both of us change over time, we hold on to an image of whom we think we are spending all of our time with rather than seeing the person he or she is becoming. That is why it is always good to retain that fresh-start approach—in any moment you can look to your lover and think, "Who is this person I share my bed with?" Becoming inquisitive in this way allows us to deepen our friendship with our spouse, as we understand her or him as a constantly changing, evolving being that is worthy of our love.

In that sense, I am reminded of something the Zen teacher Thich Nhat Hanh has said: "To love, in the context of Buddhism, is above all to be there. But being there is not an easy thing."[11] It is not easy to remember to come back continuously to this fresh-start approach, keeping an open mind and heart with your partner year after year. So my words of wisdom are based on famous advice from Seung Sahn when he spoke of holding an enlightened perspective: always don't know. In other words, always keep an inquisitive mind, a fresh-start mind, particularly when viewing your partner.

To start off a wedding ceremony, I usually like to welcome everyone who has traveled to be present for this vow. It is very special when family and friends can all gather to witness two people commit publicly to balancing each other, bringing out the best in each other, and supporting each other through all of the difficult and joyful times ahead. In essence, from a Buddhist point of view, when you get married you are committing to making your relationship a path, which denotes a recognition that things are not always easy. Being so intimate with another human being rarely is.

When we engage this path we have to acknowledge that at times the other person will rub us the wrong way. Our spouse will move the furniture or forget to change the laundry to the dryer or not call at the time he or she promised to call. Alternatively, our spouse will simply call us on our shit. The quality that makes marriage a spiritual path is learning to hold our seat in these situations and remember the ground of love and companionship that is the foundation of the relationship.

We have to learn to treat these upsets as teachings. Seung Sahn once told a story from his childhood. He said that when people wash potatoes in Korea, instead of washing them one at a time, they put them all in a tub full of water. Then someone plunges a stick into the tub, stirring the potatoes around so they rub together, knocking the dirt off one another. In that way the potatoes become clean. The same can be said for two people joining in a long-term committed relationship. When you fall into the proverbial tub together, you bump against each other, rubbing away at all the rough edges of your habitual patterns. As the dirt of habitual patterns falls away, you are rubbing away the roughness around your vulnerable and tender hearts.

When you get married within the Shambhala Buddhist tradition, there are certain tools that you are given to meditate on and actualize in order to be of benefit to yourself, your partner, your community, and the world. These tools encourage you to continuously open your heart to your partner as well as everyone you encounter. They are known as the six *paramita*s, or transcendental actions.

Param can be translated from Sanskrit to mean "other," and *ita* would be "shore." So there is a quality of transcending to another shore, beyond the river of confusion, of habitual thought, of caring only for oneself. We are talking about transcending thinking only of "me." These six tools help one to be available to others and are particularly potent when two people engage the path of marriage. Following are the six *paramitas*.

Generosity

Generosity in this context means that you are not holding on to yourself and your petty likes and dislikes. When confronted with difficult choices, you think "What would be of benefit to others?" Once you have intuited the answer to that question, you can offer whatever you have. Generosity in the context of marriage means offering yourself fully as you are to another person.

Discipline

Discipline here does not mean that you are holding yourself to a fixed set of rules, a do and don't list of how you ought to behave if you are going to be a good husband or wife. It is instead holding your mind to the view of being of benefit and acknowledging the basic goodness and wonderful qualities of your significant other.

It is the discipline that even in the toughest moments of your relationship, you bring yourself back to that perspective. Furthermore, as a couple you can take on the discipline practice of doing things properly and fully, really engaging each other, and being present for each other. These things sound simple enough, but continuing to engage these tasks over decades is a real commitment.

Patience

The third *paramita* is based on not having set expectations. It is seeing your partner as a new person every day. It is dropping your preconceived notions of what marriage should be, and how your partner should act, and experiencing the reality of who this person truly is. When you drop your set notions of how your partner should look and behave, it is hard to get impatient with her or him.

Patience in this context is not a wait-and-see approach but a commitment to be there. Sometimes that means you have to be present with strong emotions, as your partner may very well know how to push your buttons. By applying patience you learn to experience strong emotions without acting out on them. You are offering gentleness to yourself and your spouse.

Joyful Exertion

As you spend years with this partner, certain expectations and patterns become established. These are not always bad. Perhaps you like to exercise together or spend time cooking and tasting good food every Sunday. Even though you may find yourself doing the same things regularly, it is important to remain vigilant against falling into habitual ways of viewing each other.

The *paramita* of joyful exertion is based on overcoming the habitual way of relating to your spouse. It is the idea that in any moment you have the choice to engage your partner and your world fully, bringing your whole heart to it. The exertion aspect is that you need to rouse yourself beyond your normal limits to be fully present with that person and to see him or her with that fresh-start mind.

When you bring your full self to your marriage, you begin to appreciate all the details of your relationship. Those activities you regularly engage in together, such as cooking a meal, going out with friends, paying the bills, or doing your taxes, are not just ways of passing the time but opportunities to grow together spiritually. Exertion here is not viewing your life and your marriage as a hassle but joyfully engaging it to the max.

Meditation

As with all things, you are invited to bring your meditative mind to your relationship. You always have the choice to space out when spending time with your spouse or to be present with him or her. You can bring your self-reflective nature, and a willingness to be awake to life situations as they are, to your relationship.

This *paramita* is based on fresh-start mind. This is being willing to look at your life with a don't-know attitude, realizing that your partner and your relationship are always changing and meeting that change by throwing fixed mind out the window and being available to what the world and your spouse present you.

Prajna

The last *paramita* is known as *prajna*. It is a Sanskrit term. *Pra* can be translated as "super" or "superior," while *jna* is "knowing." Stringing those two words together, you see that *prajna* is superior knowledge, or wisdom. Specifically it is the type of wisdom that takes focusing on "me" and "what I need to be happy" out of the equation so you just see reality as it is.

You are not coloring your life or your relationship with fixed expectations but tuning in to how things truly are. You are not looking to see good and bad in your partner, how he or she was or ought to be, but appreciating your partner for who he or she is in this very moment. It is the ability to pay attention to this person you are spending your time with without painting her or him with your projections. You are accepting and loving your spouse with the tenderness of your open heart, your *bodhicitta*.

When you engage the six *paramitas*, you grow as a person, together you grow as a couple, and you are both able to benefit others. In fact, you unknowingly provide an incredible example for the world around you.

Within the context of a Shambhala Buddhist wedding, the couple makes offerings to a shrine that they create, bringing forth symbolic representations for each of these six *paramitas*. Essentially, each partner commits to bringing these qualities into the marriage from that moment on. Then they get to kiss.

If marriage is on your horizon, I hope that you and your partner will treat each other with gentleness, kindness, and understanding, always holding each other in your hearts with respect and compassion.

Breaking Up Is Hard to Do

> What advice would you offer about breaking up when
> you are still in love with the person?

The singer Neil Sedaka nailed it with his song "Breaking Up Is Hard to Do." Particularly if you are still in love with the person you are parting ways with, you will experience what I find to be the most aptly named emotion: heartbreak. It literally feels like your heart is physically ripping open, breaking as a result of your loss.

While any student of Buddhism may remind you that the reality of impermanence is a bitch, it's a whole other thing to feel the loss of a relationship. I empathize and know that pain. If you have been with someone for months or even years and that person simply disappears from your life, it can leave an empty hole that is hard to fill. You may try to fill it with new people to date or sleep with, or alcohol or drugs or new hobbies, but that hole is so vast that those temporary distractions seem to get lost in there.

The first piece of advice I would offer anyone going through a breakup is to sit with whatever emotions arise, without judgment. At times you may feel loss, as one of your best friends has left you and it no longer feels appropriate to talk with this person about all the details of your life. Or you may feel anger, in that your friend has done you wrong by abandoning your life together or he or she did something mean-spirited that led to the demise of the relationship. Or perhaps you just feel confusion: you have no idea what went wrong and how it all went to shit. Regardless of what you are feeling, that is okay.

The more you sit with your emotions, both on and off the meditation cushion, the easier they are to work with. It may feel like hell, but in the words of Suzuki Roshi, "Hell is not punishment, it's training." You are training to be with pain, which is great, since we have this whole cycle of suffering we seem to be immersed in and it's not as if we're never going to have to address pain again. Sakyong Mipham Rinpoche has said, "One could say that life is at least 50 percent pain. If we do not relate to pain, we are not relating to half our life."[12] Working with these strong emotions is both hell and a training ground; it is also inherently okay.

It is no surprise that you would still feel love for your ex. While love is an emotion, it is so powerful that it hangs around even when the object of your love has left. The Insight Meditation teacher and author Sharon Salzberg wrote, "Love exists in itself, not relying on owning or being owned."[13] Unlike pride or jealousy, it doesn't just vanish overnight as your mind drifts on to other things. You have habituated yourself to loving someone, to always having this person on your mind, so even though she or he may no longer be with you physically, that doesn't mean the habit is broken. Love will still exist, and that is okay.

Sometimes when people break up, they need not to be around the other person, at least for a time. Others try to maintain a friendship or at least remain on speaking terms right off the bat. Seung Sahn was once asked about this topic and said, "Being a bodhisattva means that when people come, don't cut them off; when people go, don't cut them off."[14] That means that when someone enters your life, you should not shut the person out of your heart. When someone leaves, don't shut the person out of your heart. It is disrespectful to your partner to pretend that what existed between you was not of value. That is aggression, causing harm to your ex, and is a form of ignorance that harms you as well.

Don't be surprised if you feel a wide range of emotions. A musician and gentleman I consider a very amazing Zen student, Leonard Cohen, once sang, "I'm good at love, I'm good at hate. It's in between I freeze." When your lover leaves you, you might be inclined to vacillate between these extremes. One moment you love your ex and can't live without her. The next you hate her for the pain she has caused you and never want to speak with her again. The middle ground between these two is letting the infinite number of other emotions that come up wash over you like waves. That is very hard to do. That is where most of us freeze up and forget our practice. Yet that uncomfortable, uncertain, difficult place is the training ground for working with every other emotion in our lives.

There are many ways to exist in that uncomfortable zone between love and hate. One tip Pema Chödrön has recommended is that you place a picture of your ex somewhere you will see it often. It can be in your hallway or on your refrigerator or on your desk. Whenever you see the face of your old lover, you can think to yourself, "I wish for your deepest well-being." If that phrase doesn't ring true to you, I recommend that you make one up for yourself. It could be "I wish that you find happiness" or "I wish that you will not suffer so much." As with so much of what is being discussed here, the most important thing is that you make this practice your own.

Over time, emotions change. Even the love you feel for your ex may shift over time. You can be curious about your experience as the days shift into weeks and into months after your breakup. Looking at that love you have for your ex, you can ask yourself, "Is it the same sort of love that existed when we first started dating?" Sit with that question for a moment and see what comes up.

After looking at your initial response, you can ask yourself, "Is this the same love that existed when we got into that all-night fight and I slept on the couch?" The more you explore how you feel and how you have felt in the past, the more you may realize that love, like all emotions, is a very fluid thing. You can look at what arises in your heart and conclude with the question, "What is this love that I feel today?" See if that love shifts over time. Is it different from yesterday? Is it different from last week? Last year? Remain inquisitive and without judgment.

I am always astounded by people who have loved each other as friends for years and then end up becoming romantically involved. It's as if they had one way of relating to each other and then they just did a slide to the right and all of a sudden romantic love bloomed. Perhaps later on down the road they might slide further and deepen their love and get married. Or maybe they slide in a different direction and break up. That love may dissipate or change, but that does not mean that it did not exist, in a real way, at one time and wasn't valuable for both of them.

In other words, you don't have to develop concepts about how to define a relationship with another being in order to love that person in some way. You can just practice being in love. I'm a firm believer that the more we open our hearts to others—including those who have wronged us, broken our hearts, or at times left us paralyzed with grief—the greater chance we have at achieving enlightenment. Chögyam Trungpa Rinpoche once said, "If you cannot fall in love, you cannot get enlightened."[15] Love is a beautiful and potent training ground for spiritual practice. Keeping an open heart in a difficult time is the greatest and most rewarding challenge of all.

Keeping your ex in your heart may be scary, but you have to remember that we all love love. Receiving or giving it, even in the midst of your own heartache or feeling of loss, is an incredible gift.

4 / CHANGE THE WORLD LIKE A BUDDHA

When the mob and the press and the whole world tell
you to move, your job is to plant yourself like a tree by
the river of truth and tell the whole world, "No, *you*
move."

—*Captain America*

It was when Siddhartha determinedly sat down to meditate
until he attained complete awakening that the demon king
Mara came to torment him. Mara sent his many demon sub-
jects to distract the future Buddha from his goal. As each of
the world's pleasures and pains was thrown at Siddhartha, he
easily shrugged them off, returning to his meditation practice. Finally, Mara took to poking at Siddhartha's accomplishments: "Who the fuck do you think you are?," Mara basically
said. "You think you're worthy enough of attaining enlightenment? Cool your heels, chief." I can really imagine Mara
using one of those backhanded-compliment terms like *boss* or
slugger or *chief*.

   In that moment Siddhartha could have responded in any
number of ways, but he shut up and simply touched the earth
with one hand. It is said that the earth physically shuddered
in response, bearing witness to Siddhartha's worthiness. This

single act made all of Mara's demons flee. Shortly thereafter Siddhartha became enlightened.

From that moment on Siddhartha never backed down from a fight, even though what he was doing was incredibly countercultural. His teachings upset many aspects of Indian society twenty-six hundred years ago and continue to today. He accepted people from all caste backgrounds into his monastic order, and women as well. Through doing such acts he posed a threat to Indian society as a whole. He fought for equality simply through making his teachings accessible. Those same teachings around mindfulness and compassion are still countercultural in today's speedy, aggressive, chaotic world.

One of the many fonts of wisdom within the comic world, Captain America, offers the advice in the epigraph above about how we can follow in the Buddha's footsteps by standing firm. When we are present enough that we witness suffering, we can plant ourselves firmly, like a tree by the river of truth, and say, "I won't stand for that." We can bear witness to a world in pain and respond with the kindness of an open heart.

In this chapter we will explore what it can look like to bring about social justice in today's world based on Buddhist tenets. This path is important, as we cannot ignore that everyday we have an impact on this world in one way or another. As Sakyong Mipham Rinpoche wrote, "We have entered a time when spirituality no longer means simply individual liberation—nor would that be possible, given our global connectivity."[1] We will examine how we end up causing harm when we become attached to fixed opinions and perspectives and how to join Buddhist principles with our passion for creating a better world. The view of basic goodness is that we already have everything we need to create social change. At the end of the day, it's not someone else who is going to come out of nowhere and make the world a better place. It's you. So let's get to work.

You Have to Give It All

I like the ideals of Mahayana Buddhism and like to think of myself as kind, compassionate, and giving, but in reality I'm a bit scared of all of this thinking of others first. What and how much will I have to give to be a Buddhist?

Anyone interested in being of great benefit to the world will need to give his or her heart in its totality. *Bodhisattva* is a Sanskrit term for individuals who have devoted themselves without reservation to creating positive change in the world. *Bodhi* is the same word we mentioned earlier in the context of *bodhicitta*. It means "open" or "awake." *Sattva* is being or person. It is someone willing to be open continuously. During the Dalai Lama's first visit to the United States, a photo was shot of him holding a Coca-Cola bottle. This photo was run in the local newspaper with the caption, "The Dalai Lama Takes a Break." Chögyam Trungpa Rinpoche found that event very funny. The Dalai Lama is the latest reincarnation of the bodhisattva of compassion, Avalokitesvara. Lifetime after lifetime he has come back to be helpful to others, to give of himself entirely. The idea that he is ever off duty, taking a break, is pretty ludicrous.

Similarly, if you want to be of benefit to others and follow the Mahayana path, you cannot segregate your life into specific compartments: the time I'm helping others, "me time," and the time I'm allowed to be a jerk. That's not really how it works. Chögyam Trungpa Rinpoche wrote, "The important point is to realize that you are never off duty. You can never just relax, because the whole world needs help."[2] This is not to say that you need to run around trying to fix the entire world but that everyone you encounter would benefit from your openhearted presence. There is no need to take time off from offering that.

If you think of yourself as kind, compassionate, and giving, then you know that when you invoke those qualities you give of all of yourself. When you are talking to a friend who is having a rough time, you're not sitting there thinking about all the things you wish you were doing. You're offering your full attention. You already know how to give all of yourself. You know that when you leave your friend, you feel good about that activity. So why not tread the path of the bodhisattva and do that more?

The Buddha said, "Looking after oneself, one looks after others. Looking after others, one looks after oneself."[3] You can take care of yourself to the point where compassion arises. You are able to offer your full presence because you have looked after yourself. When you do act compassionately toward others, you are also benefiting yourself. You feel good about being of benefit. You are growing as a person and as a bodhisattva in training.

You are exercising your heart muscle to see how much you can accommodate. Some days you may feel that you can lift just a little bit and are just a little more compassionate and open with other people than normal. At other times you may feel that you are taking on the pain and suffering of your entire family or group of friends and navigating that openly and genuinely. The important aspect here is to give it your all, as much as you can.

This well of *bodhi* is fathomless. It is so vast. We can always refresh ourselves from it. We have so much "awake" to give that to answer the final aspect of the question in this section, "What and how much will I have to give?," I have to say that you give it all. You leave it all out on the field. That is the practice of a bodhisattva: taking others' happiness as your own; the happiness of others makes you happy.

There is a practice that is particularly helpful on this Mahayana path. It is known as *tonglen*. This is a Tibetan term that can be translated as "sending and receiving." It is a compassion practice, where you breathe in the things that are painful or uncomfortable for others, and then when you breathe out, you send those people pleasing, soothing qualities. Whenever you see suffering in the world, you can take it to the meditation cushion through this traditional practice. There are four stages of *tonglen:*

1. Gap

To begin, sit *shamatha* for at least ten minutes. When your meditation timer goes off, raise your gaze a bit and allow yourself to experience a brief mental gap. Allow your mind to experience its own vastness. Connect to the present moment without an object of meditation.

2. Textures

As you return to focusing on your breath, begin to work with textures. As you breathe in, imagine that you are breathing in hot, heavy energy. This may feel a bit claustrophobic, which is fine. Breathe in this weightiness through every pore of your body. Then when you exhale, breathe out fresh, cool energy. If you recall those gum commercials where someone chews the gum and these wisps of fresh, minty coolness flow out of the chewer's mouth, that's basically what we are talking about. Let light, brilliant energy come out, radiating it outward. Do this practice of breathing in and out, visualizing these textures, for a few minutes.

3. Individuals

Having gotten the hang of the ebb and flow of connecting your breath to these textures, bring to mind a specific difficult circumstance. Try your hardest not to shut down your *bodhicitta* but remain open to the scenario.

I recommend starting this process by bringing to mind someone you care about deeply. It can be a family member, a friend, a pet, whatever works for you. As you breathe in, feel as if you were breathing in the person's or animal's specific pain. If your family member is struggling with drugs, you can breathe in that feeling of addiction. You may not know exactly what the person is going through, but we all know that experience of hooked craving, where we can focus only on what we desire. You can breathe that feeling in and then breathe out a sense of calm or relief or spaciousness to that person.

After a minute or two of focusing on the loved one, taking in the person's feelings of pain on the in-breath and offering up whatever comfort you can on the out-breath, move on to other people in your life for whom you want to develop compassion. You can extend this practice to other loved ones, to your neighbors or coworkers, to your dry cleaner, or to your ex-girlfriend or ex-boyfriend. All beings are worthy of our compassion, so they can all be included in *tonglen* practice.

4. Go Bigger

As you conclude working with a person during your *tonglen* practice, you can extend your practice beyond that specific scenario. For example, if your family member is indeed struggling with drugs, you can start by developing compassion for that loved one and then extend that feeling to everyone struggling with addiction. According to the National Institute on Drug Abuse, there are literally millions of people in America alone who have formed a dependency on drugs. You can breathe in the hot, heavy feelings of craving and desire and breathe out cooling, fresh feelings of relief to those people as one big group.

It is important to start at a personal level before going big. If you sit down and just contemplate how many drug addicts there are out there and attempt *tonglen* for them, you may end up with this being a theoretical exercise. If you start with your cousin, a man you see struggling on a day-to-day basis to keep his life together, it becomes real and experiential. At the end of your *tonglen* practice, return to *shamatha* for another ten minutes. Ground yourself back in the present moment by focusing on the natural flow of your breath, sans visualization.

Even if you have trouble with the visualization aspect of *tonglen*, you can recognize that the practice reverses our habitual patterns. We often want to cling to our own happiness and joy and avoid any form of other people's suffering. Here we are inverting that scenario, and with faith in our ability to manifest basic goodness, we take on others' pain and offer our positive feelings.

You don't have to do *tonglen* solely on the meditation seat. You can do it in your everyday life. When you walk past a pet store and see sad puppies in the window, you can breathe in their pain or loneliness and breathe out your own sense of contentment for a few minutes. When your coworker is freaking out about an upcoming project, you can breathe in her panic and breathe out whatever sense of calm you possess. When your family member gets sick, you can breathe in his discomfort and breathe out your own well-being. It is wise to begin training in *tonglen* practice on the meditation cushion, but after a while you may find yourself doing it naturally throughout the day.

Sometimes people are overwhelmed by *tonglen* practice. They think, "This is too much. Do I really have to relate to other people's pain? My own is already pretty intense." That is certainly not an uncommon feeling. Seung Sahn has countered this sort of question with questions of his own. He said, "How much do you believe in yourself? How much do you help other people? These are the most important questions."[4]

In fact, I would posit that contemplating Seung Sahn's questions will trump all of your own hesitations and doubts. If you want to be of benefit to other people, you must believe in yourself. You must have faith in your own basic goodness, your own capability. Having developed confidence in your ability to be openhearted, you must be willing to offer that open heart to everyone you encounter. You must help other people. That is the Mahayana view. That is the path of the bodhisattva. That is giving it your all.

Inviting Psychopaths to Your Party

How do Buddhists reconcile to the idea that psychopaths (aka sociopaths, such as Hitler, Manson, Bundy, and even your friendly neighborhood sociopath who merely kills animals for fun, or people who simply demolish friends and loved ones) may not be born with basic goodness, thereby shattering the tenet that all beings are born with basic goodness?

As unpopular as this view may be in today's world, the Buddhist perspective is that everyone is born with basic goodness. Even Hitler. Even Manson. Even Bundy. Even those messed-up people who go into schools and murder innocent people. They are all basically good. They are not inherently evil. They are so very confused. They deserve our compassion.

I believe that when people hear me speak on this topic, some of them think I am defending these individuals. I certainly am not. There are some people out there who have done some really horrendous things, things that break my heart. I am, however, defending the view that these people are basically good. During a leadership gathering in the Shambhala community, while Sakyong Mipham Rinpoche was speaking about society today, he said, "What will determine our success is the ability to remain open to the universal message [of basic goodness] and to remain unequivocal in our trust of human nature."

When you begin to engage in compassion practices such as loving-kindness contemplations or *tonglen,* you are working to drop all fixed perspectives. You are instructed not to focus your compassion solely on people you like. You have to include everyone you dislike and disagree with as well. You have to include people you don't even know, because as Sharon Salzberg has said, "In touch with your wholeness, with a heart filled with love, there is no such thing as a stranger."[5]

To return to the idea of practicing compassion for a loved one who is struggling with addiction, you are instructed to move beyond thinking of just that person and practice compassion for everyone in that plight. Everyone, in this case, includes that man who mugged you for drug money years ago and the intoxicated man who barfed on your shoes last week. "Everyone" includes people we love, people we hate, and people we don't give a fuck about.

Compassion, in this larger context, means that you have to have trust in human nature, as the Sakyong points out. Even the sick individuals who kill or otherwise harm loved ones or children can be redeemed. You have to acknowledge that even those people are just that—sick—and still have a shred of basic goodness in their being. If you can do this, then you are remaining open to the universal message of basic goodness and positively influencing society overall.

Last year I led a meditation workshop at Kripalu in Lenox, Massachusetts. The day participants arrived, tragedy struck America: twenty-eight individuals lost their lives in the Newtown, Connecticut, shooting. One man, who the media will likely claim in the long run was mentally deranged, shot and killed his mother, then went to a school and killed twenty first graders and six more of their teachers an administrators before taking his own life.

I feel now the same way I felt then, that no words can accurately describe this profound loss. These children will never grow up to meet their first loves or make an impact in their chosen profession or know the joy of being married or having kids of their own. The amazing educators who gave their lives protecting the children are such heroes; they saw an opportunity to save precious lives and took it. They are bodhisattvas.

That night I gave a short introductory talk to the participants. It was an overview on why meditation is helpful in today's world. I felt such sadness in the room that I knew it would be best if we spoke of this tragedy openly. At the end we each made an aspiration, did *tonglen,* or said a prayer for the victims of the Newtown tragedy. The next day we included them in our loving-kindness meditation practice. It was the least we could do to acknowledge this horrible occasion.

Halfway through the workshop, one of the participants approached me privately. She explained that earlier that week she was at a mall in Portland, Oregon, when yet another deranged individual had walked in and opened fire. She told me that if she had decided to get a hamburger instead of sushi, she would have turned right instead of left and walked straight into the line of fire. She could easily have been killed. She was lucky to be alive but was clearly traumatized.

She told me that she had had a breakthrough after our loving-kindness practice. "I don't forgive these shooters," she said, "but I did find myself hoping that after a life of suffering they were finally at peace." This woman's breakthrough touched me deeply. Even if you cannot summon the same level of compassion and openhearted affection for Hitler as you can for your mother, you can still wish these beings (or psychopaths) peace.

When you engage in compassion practices, you have to be open to helping everyone. In talking about committing to the Mahayana path, Pema Chödrön wrote, "Making the second commitment [to this path] means holding a diversity party in our living room, all day every day, until the end of time."[6] You cannot choose whom you invite to your compassion party. Your mother may show up, but so may Hitler. So may other people who are very confused and who act out of that confusion and harm innocent people. You have to offer the guacamole dip to all of them and invite them to take a seat.

In offering compassion to everyone, we are developing trust in basic goodness. The Sakyong, in that talk to the Shambhala leadership, said, "The result of trust is joy. Our effectiveness in helping others will be based on that trust in basic goodness. Shambhala is saying not just that humans are basically good but that society as a whole is basically good."

We are all in this society together. We cannot close our hearts to psychopaths or potential psychopaths. We have to be willing to help everyone. In fact, the potential psychopaths are the ones who need our help most of all.

We cannot say we are interested in offering our heart to this world and then pick and choose whom that includes. We need to trust in our own basic goodness as well as the goodness of everyone else we encounter. We need to trust that no matter how confused other people may be, ranging from someone acting out of jealousy at work to someone who is somehow able to slaughter children, they have basic goodness deep inside them. That is not a tenet but an experience. This trust in basic goodness is something you can experience for yourself if you are willing to host a diversity party and invite the whole world. Please have faith in your goodness and your ability to help confused people.

THE UNTOUCHABLES AND LOOSENING FIXED MIND

How would the Buddha involve himself or not involve himself in the politics, issues, and challenges of our times? For example, would he check out completely and practice in a cave? Would he be an activist? Given the challenges we face because of global warming, constant war, and the growing gap between the rich and the poor, it doesn't look like we even have a choice.

I hardly think the Buddha was a "hide out and meditate" sort of guy. He was actually a radical for his time. For example, in the midst of a highly structured class system, the Buddha accepted people from all castes into his monastic order. During the Buddha's lifetime there was a social caste known as the untouchables. While the name sounds like it's intended for a tough street gang, it was actually a whole group of people who were deemed literally not worthy of being touched by other classes. The view was that if you came too close to an untouchable, the person would pollute you.

One such untouchable man, Sunita, was a road sweeper. As part of his caste obligations, whenever he saw someone of a higher caste come down the street, he would have to run and hide. One day when the Buddha was coming down the street, Sunita could not find a good hiding place. The Buddha spotted him, looking terrified, and approached him. The Buddha asked, "My dear friend, would you like to leave this work and follow me?" At first Sunita tried to explain his caste situation, but the Buddha's invitation stood. "On our path, we no longer distinguish between castes. You are a human being like the rest of us." Overwhelmed by how humble and gracious the Buddha was, Sunita joyfully accepted and became a monk.

As you can imagine, news of the Buddha's accepting an untouchable into his order spread wide and fast. By accepting everyone, the Buddha had thrown down a sword, cutting through the systemic class order of the time. Some members of the higher castes went so far as to accuse the Buddha of attempting to overthrow the existent class system entirely.

The Buddha remained unperturbed by these rumors, though, remarking that his way was one of equality and that future generations would look back at this act as social progress. He was right (as usual). Sunita became so adept a meditator and teacher that even kings and other members of the highest castes came to respect him.

The story of Sunita is just one of many describing how the Buddha took a leap of faith in others' goodness, despite the unpopularity of this level of social equality at the time. While I don't think the Buddha ever intentionally set out to uproot the social norms of his day, this path of being openhearted and mindful seems to fly in the face of societal conventions; there was never any question of his playing down any of the work he intended to do in the name of equality just because other people wouldn't like it.

In that sense, I believe that anyone who is interested in being an activist, getting involved in politics, or simply trying to help out in her or his own neighborhood should follow in the Buddha's footsteps. You can connect with your vast and open heart, reach out to help everyone you encounter, and lead by example in working for equality for all. In speaking about societal change, Sakyong Mipham Rinpoche has said that if people in leadership have confidence in their individual basic goodness, then this will shift our culture overall.

The Sakyong quoted his father, Chögyam Trungpa Rinpoche, when he remarked, "Society is the psychological environment of a group." He went on to acknowledge that we all have an opportunity to be of benefit to society simply by trusting in basic goodness. If we can shift our own perspective to align with our experience of basic goodness and act from that perspective, then we will have a strong influence over everyone we encounter. We will be able to shift the psychological environment around us through our very presence.

This strong influence is not based on running out into the world and trying to force "me" and "my view of how things ought to be" on others. Forcing fixed views on other people is just another form of aggression. Society does not need more aggression. Instead, we are talking about opening our heart wide enough to accommodate everyone we encounter as part of our path.

If you want to shift the psychological environment of a group, you have to do it from a place of openness rather than from your own sense of what is right and wrong. You have to give up all of those fixed expectations and opinions and relax enough to see the way things truly are. You must be awake to reality as it is. Pema Chödrön wrote, "Awakening is not a process of building ourselves up but a process of letting go."[7] Part of being awake is checking your fixed mind at the door. It is letting go of the way you think things ought to be and seeing the psychological environment as it is.

The more you are able to let go of your fixed mind, the more you will be able to find joy within this present moment.

Leonard Cohen once sang, "The less there was of me, the happier I got." If you want to be happy, apply your meditation practice to your work in creating societal change. You can be interested in supporting antipoverty legislation, creating community gardens in your neighborhood, or having your company use more ecofriendly resources; all of your work for good can fall under the umbrella of being present and expressing your innate goodness.

Let your ability to be present inform your actions. Be with what is as opposed to how you wish things were. When you rest with what is, you will see the most skillful way to act. You will be able to tap in to your basic goodness and let your open heart transform the world. Just as the Buddha did, you can create incredible social change just by being open enough to accept all beings into your heart equally.

THE POWER OF LOVE AND ROLE MODELS

I feel that there aren't a lot of role models for creating change in today's world. There were people like Martin Luther King Jr. and Mahatma Gandhi, but who fills those roles in today's scene? What is the Buddhist view of finding (or maybe being) that sort of person?

In every generation there are a handful of people that we look to and say, "That person did so much to create positive change in the world." The Martin Luther King Jr.'s and the Mahatma Gandhis of the world are good examples of that. Yet for every one of those well-known figures, a thousand more bodhisattvas work humbly in their lives and create a tremendous difference without the world's ever knowing who they are. I believe you can be one of those people. I believe that because I have had the good fortune to know such a person.

On July 13, 2012, the twenty-nine-year-old long-time Obama staffer Alex Okrent died unexpectedly of heart failure while working at his desk. I was Alex's best friend, and on a personal note, his death has left me devastated. I live a devastated life as a result of my best friend's passing. In the aftermath of his death, Alex was honored in many ways: the president and vice president called his family, eight hundred people came to his funeral service, and his life and legacy were written up widely.

At the time of this writing, I am still mentally processing a wonderful article written by Mark Leibovich in the *New York Times Magazine*. As part of their "The Lives They Lived" annual retrospective, Mr. Leibovich interviewed many of Alex's close friends and family members. The article he subsequently developed was included alongside twenty-one others honoring notable people who passed away this last year, such as Whitney Houston and Neil Armstrong.

At this point you may wonder "Why Alex? Why was he such a big deal?" To be honest, it's taken me some time to figure that out, as I'm a bit too close to the situation myself. He did work for one of the more historic presidential campaigns of our time. He did die prematurely. But at the end of the day, he was so well known within that world because he was so loving. Alex was a big deal, a role model of sorts, because he was a loving man.

Alex was with the Obama campaign starting when Barack was running for the senate. As he became more and more involved in the administration and the 2008 and 2012 campaigns, his warmth, humor, and passion touched many people. He would recommend people he met for positions within the organization and go out of his way to cheer up coworkers or provide them with as many resources as possible so they could do their job effectively. Whenever possible, he would lean in and attempt to connect to other people in a genuine and fearless manner.

Alex was always willing to be there, fully, for anyone he encountered. After we graduated from college I went to work for meditation centers and practiced compassion in that context. Alex went into the world of politics and found his own way of being openhearted in that chaotic, stormy arena. Since he was available and always willing to be helpful to others, I came to regard him as a true bodhisattva.

A few days before the *New York Times* retrospective, there was a roundtable discussion on MSNBC about that issue of the magazine. Alex was mentioned as someone who gave his all for something he believed in, and the commentator mentioned that it was "profoundly unfair" that Alex never got to see Barack Obama reelected in 2012. This term, *profoundly unfair*, really struck me. In that moment the commentator and I adopted two entirely different perspectives. While he thought it was profoundly unfair that Alex wasn't around to witness the election results, I immediately thought how profoundly unfair it was that he would never do the many things he wanted to do: get married, have children, find out what he was really meant to do for a career.

I caught myself in this moment of being hooked by our divergent views and thought, "Huh. This attachment to two different perspectives is how a lot of harm is caused in this world. We come from the same idea and go in two different directions, and now I feel at odds with someone I've never met." Then I dropped the fixed point of view I was attached to and came back to listening to this commentator.

You may have a particular issue you think is profoundly unfair. You might have a passion for environmental issues or want to be an antipoverty advocate or believe that more accessible education is the way to build the future of your country. You may think that the way the current system is running is profoundly unfair and want to do something about it. If you can drop your fixed point of view and engage in that issue with an open heart, you are more likely to create positive change.

The good news is that from a Buddhist perspective, when we witness suffering we are not supposed to simply sit there and gawk at it. Compassion is an active verb: we can and should leap in as bodhisattvas and make a difference in today's world. You may begin to work on a particular issue and find role models within it. You may never have known these people existed before you got involved; they are not making the *New York Times* or being quoted widely on Twitter, but they are doing amazing work even within your local community. Those are people worth working with and emulating.

Alex was not the top manager for the Obama campaign. He did not run the show. He was not the most highly paid or widely quoted. But he was one of the most loving people, and he is now widely known for that quality. This book is dedicated to Alex's memory. I have founded an institute to perpetuate his loving, authentic leadership style through other young people. He was a man who created social change through love and helped everyone he encountered simply by being there for them. May we all have so large an impact on the world and be celebrated for the love we share. May we be the role models this world needs by showing our love effortlessly and freely.

Vegetarianism and Interdependence

What is the Buddhist view of eating meat? Would the Buddha be a vegetarian today?

The simplest (and perhaps most satisfying) answer is yes. I believe that if he lived in today's world, the Buddha would be a vegetarian. When he became a buddha, he was pretty clear that the first of the five main precepts of his monastic disciples should be "I undertake a vow to abstain from taking life." He knew that every time his gigantic sangha walked to a new location, they would crush thousands of small insects underneath their feet, but his intention was that each of them should, as much as is humanly possible, avoid killing.

The surprising thing is that the no-meat stance is not generally agreed upon within the various lineages of Buddhism, despite that precept. This is a great example of how the Buddha's teachings morph and change from culture to culture, century after century, to mesh with modern times. Theravadin schools say that the Buddha allowed his monastic students to eat pork, chicken, and beef if the animal was not killed for the purpose of providing food specifically for them. And that was just for monastics; laypeople could eat whatever sort of elephant or horse meat they could find. So to be clear: the act of eating meat was deemed karmically neutral. The act of killing or having something killed for you to eat was karmically negative.

Over time, though, many savvy consumers have raised a finger and said, "But what about supply and demand?" At first it may appear that the Buddha did not buy in to that particular logic when making this decision. Since alms were basically leftovers from lay households, it was argued that the meat was not directly linked to the monks' or nuns' karma.

It's as if I showed up at your home the day after Thanksgiving and you gave me whatever leftover turkey you were putting in the fridge. By this argument I could take whatever you gave me and not be karmically responsible. Some people may find that argument convincing. I myself think that it's a bit of a cop-out; if I eat the last of your turkey, who is to say you won't wake up the next day, wish it were still there, and go out and get another one?

The reason this question falls into our category on social change is that we have to realize just how interdependent each of our decisions truly is. If you walk into a restaurant and ask for a turkey sandwich, you're not just asking for a sandwich. You are having an impact on the life of the waiter, the people in the kitchen preparing your food, the farmer who raises the turkey, the turkey (obviously), and the entire bread company with its millions of employees who rely on people like you to want to eat sandwiches, and many more lives. It's never as simple as a turkey sandwich.

Over time different schools of Buddhism have recognized this interdependence and placed various levels of importance on observing vegetarianism. Certain Vajrayana practices within Tibetan Buddhism actually call for the consumption of meat.

Add this religious context to the existing cultural one (it's incredibly hard to grow vegetables in Tibet, whereas yaks are all over the place) and you develop a certain flexibility for those monastics.

Tibetan Buddhists generally respect the "three-hand" rule, where it is a neutral act if the meat is slaughtered by one person, sold to another, and cooked by another before it reaches you. The belief here is that it has passed through three other sets of hands, so you are not personally related to the death of the animal. Even His Holiness the Dalai Lama continues to eat meat. While some people have taken him to task for doing so, he has stated that his doctors have recommended it and continues to be a carnivore while still imploring other Buddhists to become vegetarians.

While I understand someone's having to eat meat for health reasons, I think that in modern Western society it's not too hard to be a vegetarian. I think if the Buddha were with us in the West today and was not collecting alms but held a job and bought all of his own meals, he would likely choose a falafel sandwich over a Big Mac. I personally believe that he would hold the life of animals in such high regard that he would go out of his way to be a vegetarian.

As with everything else on this spiritual path, we need to determine what makes sense for us. Years ago, while discussing becoming vegetarian with my girlfriend at the time, she pointed out that I was not the best chef in the world. I have yet to learn how to cook regular, nutritious vegetarian meals for myself but want to pursue that further. While I am still on the fence about going cold turkey (pun intended), I do intend to be more mindful of my meat intake, relying on meatless options more readily. For me, that is what makes sense for now.

During a discussion many years ago, a student asked Suzuki Roshi if he ate meat. "Yes, I do," he replied. The student got angry and responded, "Buddha didn't eat any meat." Suzuki Roshi responded, "Yes, Buddha was a very pious man." I hope that sheds some initial light on the subject of vegetarianism and that you take the time to contemplate how pious you would like to be in this regard.

ABORTION AND FORGIVENESS

> I am a single mother raising my young son, who is four years old. I am forty-one, and I have been pregnant three times. The first I terminated and cannot forgive myself for. The second was a miscarriage. Every day I wonder why I am here and how I could have been so selfish as to kill my child. I love my son but wonder why I have been given another chance. I have also been very self-destructive in trying to find forgiveness for my actions. Any advice?

Generally speaking it is believed in Buddhism that life starts at the time of conception. Given the belief in reincarnation, it is said that a being dies and travels between six realms of existence before taking on a new rebirth. Little In-Between-Realms sees your parents having sex, thinks it looks pretty cool, and goes to investigate. At that point your consciousness has entered that realm and goes about the process of being born. Given that traditional idea, the Buddha taught that abortion is in fact taking a being's life, which is a grave misdeed.

In our modern world many Buddhist teachers have adjusted that position and said that there are times when it may not be a bad idea to have an abortion, such as when a child poses a significant health risk to the mother. Along those lines His Holiness the Dalai Lama was quoted in an interview with the *New York Times* as saying that "abortion should be approved or disapproved according to each circumstance." I appreciate this admission in that it seems to keep in line with the Buddha's initial invitation for us to explore his teachings and come and see for ourselves how to apply them. I find an interesting paradox on this topic. Buddhism from twenty-six hundred years ago may discourage abortion, but it also discourages imposing rigid moral absolutes.

Buddhism is such an individualistic path. I have no idea why the woman who wrote this question had an abortion and as such have no right to condemn or praise her. Instead, all I can do is think about what I might do in a similar situation. I encourage anyone contemplating this issue to take time to reflect on the motivation behind your stance. Contemplate whether your actions will diminish suffering not only for yourself but also for the child that you would be bringing into the world. As with all things, if you wish to keep in line with the nature of the Buddha's words, take the action that causes the least amount of suffering.

There is an added element to this question, which is to seek forgiveness for when you have caused suffering. The Tibetan Buddhist teacher Dilgo Khyentse Rinpoche once said, "In the case of an abortion, . . . if the parents feel remorse, they can help by acknowledging it, asking for forgiveness, and performing ardently the purification practice of Vajrasattva."[8]

Vajrasattva practice is a Tibetan Buddhist purification meditation. The word *vajra* can be translated from the Sanskrit as "indestructible" or "adamantine." The word *sattva* is the same one as in *bodhisattva;* it means "being." Vajrasattva is considered an indestructible being. What is indestructible about him? His purity.

Vajrasattva is visualized as a youthful prince whose skin is as white as pure snow. He is the essence of wisdom and awakeness. The visualization practice of Vajrasattva includes contemplating the impure actions and deeds you have undertaken as well as any emotional, mental, or physical impurities, and while reciting a mantra you visualize your body being slowly cleansed of the impurities. By the end of the session you visualize yourself possessing the same pristine nature as Vajrasattva, recognizing that your karmic acts can be purified and that at your core you are essentially good and awake.

I should clarify that Vajrasattva practice should be learned from an authorized teacher in a Vajrayana tradition. The term *vajrayana* can be translated from Sanskrit as "indestructible vehicle." It is the path of looking at every obstacle and challenge in our world as an opportunity to experience our innate goodness and see the world as sacred. Pema Chödrön commented on this unique path: "There's not a drop of rain or a pile of dog poop that appears in your life that isn't the manifestation of enlightened energy, that isn't a doorway to sacred world."[9] With the proper view and training, even the hardest things we have to go through, such as incredibly difficult medical decisions, can be a doorway to sacredness.

Dilgo Khyentse Rinpoche went on to speak about remorseful parents, saying, "They can also offer lights, and save lives, or help others, or sponsor some humanitarian or spiritual project, dedicating it to the well-being and future enlightenment of the baby's consciousness."[10] For many people who are not going to pursue Vajrasattva practice, this seems like good advice. When you feel remorse about something, often you do not have the luxury of snapping your fingers and making things different. However, you always have the chance to do good in the world. You can always do good. So anytime you feel remorse, consider helping others, sponsoring a project that will be of benefit, and acknowledge that you hope it will somehow aid beings related to whatever you feel sorry about.

While not at all in the same context or on the same scale, I am reminded of the story of the Buddha and Angulimala. Angulimala was a mass murderer. It's said that he had killed 999 people and wore a necklace of fingers, one from each of his victims. Still the Buddha went down the road to see him. Angulimala warned him that if he came any closer the Buddha would be his one thousandth victim.

The Buddha, willing to offer his life to fulfill Angulimala's desire to complete his necklace, asked only for one last wish. His only desire was for Angulimala to cut a branch from a tree. Angulimala did so and offered it to the Buddha. Then the Buddha asked him to reattach it to the tree. When he saw that the murderer was confused, the Buddha explained, "If you cannot create, you have no right to destroy. If you cannot give life, you don't have the right to give death to any living thing."

Angulimala was instantly transformed by the Buddha's wisdom; he put down his sword and was accepted into the monastic order. He was forgiven by the Buddha for his misdeeds and is said to have died a truly awakened man. I mention this story from the life of the Buddha to highlight that even the harshest and most senseless of acts can and has been forgiven. If Angulimala can transform his life and become awake, certainly anyone else can. That includes this woman who made the choice to have an abortion.

Furthermore, our largest mistakes serve as the largest fodder for our path to enlightenment. We learn which aspects of our life we want to cultivate and which we need to learn to reject. We grow stronger knowing that we have survived our mistakes and learned from them.

The person who asked this question about abortion mentioned that she had done many self-destructive things on her path toward forgiveness. The fact that she has recognized those things as destructive is the first step toward waking up. Step two is abandoning those things. Step three is even harder. Step three is learning new habits, specifically learning to be with emotions as they are, be they guilt, anger, or sadness. Feeling our emotions fully is, in my experience, the best road to forgiving ourselves for our mistakes.

The Buddha said, "If you cannot create, you have no right to destroy. If you cannot give life, you don't have the right to give death to any living thing." His words resonate with me in this particular case. At this point our question asker has given life to a precious being. She can love him and raise him with a heart full of compassion and understanding. I personally believe that parenting is a full and rich path that, if done correctly and if partnered with meditation, can lead to great awakening.

Working with Other People's Anger

How do you practice the dharma when someone's coming at you yelling and screaming and probably intending to hurt you and compassion seems impossible?

—Yankees fan at a Red Sox game

I don't often keep the names of the people who ask me questions included in my work, but this one was too good to pass up. As a former Bostonian who was born in New York City, I know just how passionate Red Sox fans can be during Yankees games. This is a different form of passion from the one I mentioned in the introduction of this chapter.

Passion in this context is a form of *shenpa*. If you recall from before, *shenpa* is a particular type of strong emotion, one that has gotten its hooks into us to the point where we feel very much attached to it. *Shenpa* in this case is not "I feel passionate about helping others," it is "I need other people to believe what I believe. Until they do I will not be happy." Passion in this context is not about feeling something strongly, it is letting that emotion take the steering wheel of your mind and drive you off a cliff to your own destruction.

At one point Chögyam Trungpa Rinpoche was watching soccer. He saw the thousands of people packed into the stadium, cheering for their chosen team to win. He turned to one of his students and said, "Look. They have been playing this game for hundreds of years." Obviously he was not referring to these two particular soccer teams. He was referring to the overall state of choosing one thing you like, which puts you in a dualistic position where you have to dislike the other thing, and you then tie your happiness to the outcome of what happens between them. That dualistic perspective has been propagated in sports, religion, and elsewhere for millennia.

The soccer example is apt, though, because some people do tie a great deal of their happiness to how their favorite sports team is doing. For a Yankees fan at a Red Sox game, this scenario of actual physical violence, or at least the threat of it, is not unheard of. Boston people love their Red Sox. I'm a fan myself. However, I realize that if I tie my happiness to whether the Red Sox win or lose, I am essentially binding myself to a roller coaster of emotions that I don't have any control over. I myself am playing that game that we have all been playing for hundreds of years, known as dualistic thinking.

You too might find that you have been playing this game of "us" versus "them." Even if you are not a big sports fan, it might show up in other areas of your life. Pema Chödrön has written, "The issue isn't with preferences but with the shenpa behind them."[11] She went on to point out that you can oppose something like gay marriage, and that is a preference. However, if you are vitriolic to every gay person you meet, that is a sign that you have been hooked by *shenpa*. You are no longer saying that you have preferences but allowing those preferences to take control of your life and perpetuate violent emotions such as anger. It is important for each of us to explore how we get hooked by *shenpa* and how that might hold us back from making a positive difference in this world.

If you are being physically attacked, though, you are a very real victim of *shenpa*, in this case someone else's *shenpa*. If you have the time and space, then ideally you can talk to the person in a clear way, conversing from an open heart, in an attempt to help the person get unhooked from her or his strong emotions. If you can remain open in the face of aggression, you have a good chance of calming the situation down.

If someone is not willing to talk, you may need to step away from the situation. When someone is hooked by anger, whether it's over losing a sports game or a loved one, you can indulge that emotion or you can step out of its way. Suzuki Roshi wrote, "To give your sheep or cow a large, spacious meadow is the way to control him. So it is with people: first let them do what they want, and watch them. This is the best policy. To ignore them is not good; that is the worst policy. The second worst is trying to control them. The best one is to watch them, just to watch them, without trying to control them."[12]

Let's break Roshi's advice down a bit. When someone is spiraling out with anger, one way to approach the scenario is just to watch and learn how the person is behaving and why. This is a good policy because you can take the time to understand why the person is acting the way he or she is and ground yourself in the present moment, the reality of the situation. Having done that, you will be best able to determine the skillful means to bring this person out of his or her anger.

Suzuki Roshi's advice is not to ignore the person or think that he or she is not worthy of your compassion. When you see someone who has been hooked by anger, that person should become the most important person in the world to you. No one needs to experience the power of an open heart more than someone who is suffering from anger. You should pay close attention to that person.

Similarly, you cannot try to control someone hooked by anger. You can try to give the person a lot of support and space so that she or he can calm down and be able to listen to what you have to say. Initially, however, an angry person only hears what is going through her or his own mind. So you have to avoid any tendency to steer that person in one direction or another because the person likely will not be able to hear your commands.

To simply watch and wait for the best time to act is a hard thing to ask of you. But you can offer your kind and open heart in any scenario, especially when you are feeling attacked. The Dalai Lama once said, "Be kind whenever possible. It is always possible." Whenever you feel attacked, be it by someone at work shooting down your ideas or belittling you or your ex publicly humiliating you or someone expressing anger over your sports team, try to be kind. Drop your *shenpa* and see and try to understand the person's own hooked emotional reaction. Step outside the dualistic context of "me" versus "them" and just be open, without conditions. Unconditional kindness can cut through aggression like a knife through butter. If all else fails, duck.

Struggling with Being "Right"

> I get really angry when I watch CNN or read *Huffington Post,* mostly because I think everyone is an idiot! It makes me feel like a bad person to feel so angry, but I know on some level I'm right. What should I do??!

The short answer to this question is "drop fixed mind." As I mentioned earlier, any time we start to think that our particular thoughts, emotions, or opinions are right and someone else's are wrong, we are setting ourselves up for conflict. The world does not need more conflict. It needs intimacy.

In his book *Awake in the World,* the meditation and yoga teacher Michael Stone said, "Enlightenment is intimacy. We are ready for true awakening when we dissolve the self-made horizons that segregate what is 'mine' and what is 'yours' and instead stay close to the basic character of ongoing change and nonattachment."[13] I think it is interesting that Michael chose to equate enlightenment with intimacy. Meditation is a very intimate practice. You are becoming so familiar with your mental ins and outs, your highs and lows, and how you get hooked by them and can free yourself from doing so. In that sense, the more intimate you are with your own mind, the more awake you will be.

The second half of Michael's words shows us that there is a big obstacle to this level of intimacy, namely dualistic mind. Dualistic mind is when we sit down on a bus or train and think "This is my seat. I hope no one else will sit next to me." Upon taking our seat we automatically put up all sorts of barriers around our *bodhicitta*. We want our own space, and anyone who tries to invade it is an enemy, an anonymous "other" whom we need to defend our territory against. Instead, we can acknowledge that someone may very well sit next to us at some point on one of our trips and loosen our attachment to what we need to be happy.

Last year I worked in Columbus, Ohio, for a number of months serving as a field organizer for the Obama presidential campaign. Campaign hours are very long and very hard. You wake up, take a shower, answer your initial e-mails, then rush to work for fourteen or sixteen hours, eating whatever is within your office or is offered to you by volunteers, and then you rush home to get a little bit of sleep before the next day.

Many of us stayed with families of ardent volunteers who would generously take us into their spare bedrooms for months on end. So when we got home after working a long and full schedule, devoting ourselves to something we thought was important and would have a major impact on society, we didn't get "me time" at the end of the day. We got time we spent with a family that was not actually ours but kindly treated us as such. I don't know what your family is like, but my experience in this regard was that this was not necessarily "down time." I also lived and worked with my dear friend Miranda, whom I cherish, but we would commute to and from work together, so even then I was not alone.

One morning I was showering and realized that the ten minutes I spent soaping up was the longest amount of waking time I had alone each day. The funny thing is, even though I wasn't eating or sleeping particularly well, I felt more invigorated than I had in a very long time. Because I had relinquished my need for privacy and what I thought I needed to be happy, I found happiness anew through service to others.

If I had decided to make my political work, my form of creating social change at that time, all about me and my ideas for how things should be, I would have spent a lot of time being miserable. There were a lot of seemingly odd individuals who volunteered for the campaign, and I spent all of my time with them. It never occurred to me to think, "Oh, David is wrong about that political idea, where we should march to D.C. and overthrow the government. I should correct him and show him the way." I had dedicated my waking hours in service to these people and our shared work and found that it was much easier to do the work and live a life with meaning if I didn't segregate the world into who is right and who is wrong (and that extended to party preferences). That would not be a way to create intimacy with others or with my world. That is a way to feed dualistic thinking.

Chögyam Trungpa Rinpoche pointed out, "We don't want to become tricky warriors, with all kinds of tricks up our sleeves and ways to cut people's logic down when we don't agree with them. Then there is no cultivation of either ourselves or others. When that occurs, we destroy any possibilities of enlightened society."[14] If you want to live in an enlightened society, a society based on mindfulness and compassion, then the way to get there is not to cut down other people, even if they are major media conglomerates. I am not defending CNN or *Huffington Post*, but I know that getting mad at them from the confines of your home is not really going to be a way to create positive change in the world.

Instead of becoming a tricky warrior, you can become a bodhisattva, an openhearted warrior. Here the term *warrior* is not about someone who goes to war, storming CNN headquarters and demanding they stop being idiots. A warrior in this context is someone who is willing to be brave and look at his or her own aggression. Instead of cutting down other people and their opinions when we don't agree with them, we look at the aggression that sprouts up in response to those opinions and cut through that. You can respond with kindness and an open heart, which furthers intimacy between you and the object of your aggression as well as between you and your own mind.

The more you can drop the idea of what you need to be happy, the happier you will be. The more you can relax into supporting movements that you believe are being of benefit to others, the more you will find you have energy and openness to offer to those movements. This process begins at home. Sakyong Mipham Rinpoche wrote, "In our households, if we foster values based on goodness—like patience and humor—they will flow into our relationships with others in our communities, eventually influencing our nations, and finally, the rest of the world."[15] The more you drop fixed mind and are open to what is, the more intimate you will become with your mind and your world. The more intimate you become with your mind and world, the closer you will be to being fully awake.

SPENDING THAT DOUGH

I think our financial system is corrupt and unfair. What would a modern-day Buddha say about money?

Money is money. It is not good or bad. It is a tool, like a hammer. You can use a hammer to put a nail in a wall and hang up art or to beat someone's brains in. However, money is unlike a hammer in that every time you engage money, you are interacting with a complex financial system. So let us explore the interdependence of money.

For years I have worked with homeless youth on a volunteer basis and have through them plugged in to the injustices that take place in the shelter system. I have friends who work in some of the hardest teaching conditions in New York City, and through them I have been exposed to a variety of problems within our educational system. I have also become friendly with local politicians in my city, and through them I have become more familiar with the "dark money" of Wall Street and our political systems. At the end of the day, I can't help but feel that we have created a great deal of organization to institutionalize suffering. The financial system is a perfect example of that.

The Buddha taught extensively about interdependence. To return to our example of ordering a turkey sandwich, we can analyze how each of our dealings has waves of impact throughout the world. We are a consumer society. Many of us spend money every day. I think the Buddha might encourage us to limit our consumption habits and to watch how quickly we get attached to the idea that we need the latest iProduct, to eat at the fanciest new restaurant, or to buy that beautiful pair of shoes. The more intimate we become with our mind, the more we start to cut through that attachment to what "I" need to make "me" happy.

At the same time, I imagine the Buddha would acknowledge that you will spend money at some point in time and offer advice on how to do that with mindfulness and compassion. Here are four suggestions for how to make money a part of your spiritual journey as opposed to something you might need to shy away from or overcome.

Discernment

Try this simple exercise: take one hundred dollars out of your bank account and just watch how you spend it. This sounds easy enough, but how many times have you gone out with friends, woken up the next day, checked your pockets, and thought, "How did I spend all of that money?" If you want, you can jot down how much you spend over the time you go through that hundred dollars. See if you are more or less discerning now that you are bringing your full attention to your spending habits.

As you continue to examine your spending patterns, you can bring your attention to which habits feel good (maybe offering a few dollars to a homeless woman) and which do not feel so good (maybe buying an overpriced but not so nutritious meal). In either case, just observe your financial dealings and see how they make you feel. Explore your habits wholeheartedly and begin to discern if there are some you want to pursue more and some you want to get rid of.

Look at Cause and Effect

Whenever you spend your money, you are creating major ramifications within a financial system that, at least in the mind of our question asker, is corrupt and unfair. With each purchase you can reinforce support for that system or move against it. Having discerned which spending habits seem to bring us peace and which cause us strife, we can apply the discipline of following through and spend our money in ways we deem meaningful. Instead of spending your money on an impulse buy that you get bored with days later, you might find that you get more gratification from donating that money to a cause you believe in.

Khenpo Tsultrim Gyamtso Rinpoche is known for his spontaneous verses of realization. One such verse goes

> Working very hard so that your wealth will accrue
> Then you guard it so well—how much anxiety this all
>   brings you!
> To get rid of it, remember this a lot
> Wealth is dreamlike, whether you have or have not
> When you know material things to be just a dream
> You'll be enriched by contentment, of all wealth
>   supreme.[16]

Here Rinpoche points out that if you hoard your wealth, you will find yourself lost in anxiety. Counting your money has never made anyone other than Scrooge McDuck happy. Instead, you can try to implement the *paramita* of generosity and offer your money in ways that you feel will have a positive effect on the world. Money will come and money will go, but if you use it in a way that helps others, then you will undoubtedly feel contentment.

Examine the Essence of Money

One aspect of Khenpo Tsultrim Gyamtso Rinpoche's advice to us is that we examine the very nature of money itself. He calls it dreamlike, pointing us toward the traditional Buddhist teachings around change and emptiness. Here emptiness is not the sense of

a mug of tea being half empty but that the very nature of our bodies and our worlds is that they are not as solid as we might think.

Earlier we looked at how ephemeral our emotions can be.
Applying the same level of scrutiny to the rest of our lives, we
can see how our bodies change and evolve constantly. We can
see that our parents are getting older and their minds and bodies are changing too. Our childhood neighborhood, our favorite bar, and our brand-new car change over time. Everything
around us, all phenomena, is constantly fluctuating. Nothing is
as real and solid as we give it credit for. It is empty of permanent, lasting nature.

The truth of emptiness is evident in our financial structure. America was considered economically superior for many
years. At the time of this writing, that is no longer the case.
People had thought that their investments would continue to
increase over time, that they would forever have access to good
jobs, and that they would be able to pay their mortgages. Then
our bubble burst and a new reality, one based on a recession,
was revealed. This was a big shock to everyone but particularly
so for people who had set ideas about their financial picture.
The idea that their money was subject to change (in a very negative sense) was surprising to say the least.

On a more individual level, money has become more
ephemeral for each of us as our technology has increased. It
used to be that you could pay for things only with cash, credit
cards, or check. Now you can use Web sites to pay for things,
buy items with one-click shopping, and pay your bills electron-
ically. The only way you might track your financial picture is
by going to the Web site for your bank and looking at a number
stating your account balance. That feels very evanescent to me.
It seems silly to attach your very well-being to whatever number is on the computer screen that day. You are more than that
number; you are more than your money.

When you find yourself becoming attached to your money,
give that attachment up. It comes and goes. Money cannot hurt
you; only our attachment to it can. It is up to you whether you

get hooked by your emotional reactions to the ever-changing reality of your financial situation. If you do, you will be plagued by anxiety. If you don't, you will find contentment. This idea is not just about money, of course, but is applicable to all of our external circumstances.

Wield Your Money Appropriately

With conviction of your awake state, your basic goodness, you can infuse simple transactions throughout your day with a quality of joy and contentment. You are basing your financial interactions on your ability to be kind, compassionate, and capable, so you are wielding your money as skillfully as a samurai would his sword.

When you take the view that you will make all of your financial decisions in line with your own goodness, then you are recognizing money as a tool for your spiritual journey. You are taking the interplay between you and your world as an inherently sacred experience, and your money is the conduit of expressing your wakefulness. Instead of looking to money as something that is just part of a corrupt or unfair system, you use it to better yourself and others, which is a magical act.

Because we live within a society, we have the choice to go with how others do things in that society or go a different route and try something new. When you try something new, you are making an impact on that society. Here you can acknowledge that our financial system is not great but spend your own money in a way that is counter to the consumer culture we live in. You can use it as the warrior's weapon, helping others to the best of your ability.

You can be discerning with how you spend your money. You can watch how it affects others and adjust your spending habits to make sure you have the largest positive impact. Throughout that process you can acknowledge money's ephemeral nature and wield it with confidence in your basic goodness. The result of this process is that you are showing that money can be a manifestation of enlightened energy. You are treating money as a doorway, opening up your life to a sacred world.

Just Give Peace a Chance

> Do Buddhists really believe that if they and everybody else would just be kind to one another there truly could be peace on earth? Isn't that a little naive?

Not really. Imagine for a moment that all the people of the world did, even for a day, put down their aggression and the tools of their aggression (guns, knives, drones, tanks) and were simply kind to whomever they encountered. We would have, even if only for a day, world peace. You may think me naive in wishing for that, but if we did all practice kindness, in every aspect of our lives, we would live in a wonderfully peaceful world.

The naive aspect may be that we are so far from that reality that my "lay down your weapons" plan feels too unattainable. Today it may be. But tomorrow is a new day. This is a dream, I admit. But there was once a man who fell from the planet Krypton and landed here on earth who believed in dreams. The comic book character Superman once said, "Dreams save us. Dreams lift us up and transform us. And on my soul, I swear . . . until my dream of a world where dignity, honor, and justice becomes the reality we all share—I'll never stop fighting." I can't speak for Buddhists worldwide, but for my part I feel emboldened by the dream of worldwide kindness and will continue to strive, in my own way, for kindness to spread like the world's best virus.

It was Gandhi who said, "Peace between countries must rest on the solid foundation of love between individuals." I am not so naive as to think that world peace will come from wishful thinking. It will come from people learning to love fully. The first step there is learning self-love, and then learning to embrace everyone, from your mother to Hitler, with that same love. I agree with Gandhi that if we can overcome our own emotional warfare and learn to love, then we will have a great impact on society. If everyone in a country learned to love, peace would be born.

The Shambhala tradition takes its name from a story that originated at the time of the Buddha. A great king, Dawa Sangpo, had heard of the Buddha and wanted to meet him. He probably Googled him, watched some of his YouTube clips, and was, like, "I gotta check this guy out." So Dawa Sangpo goes in search of the Buddha but feels a little let down when he realizes that in order to study with him he will need to become a monk.

Dawa Sangpo approached the Buddha and explained his situation. "I've got this whole kingdom back home expecting me to rule them," he said. "I can't just walk away from that; it's irresponsible." The Buddha is said to have sent his monastic followers out of the room and imparted what is known as the Kalachakra teachings to Dawa Sangpo. The king was then able to return home and lead his kingdom based on these teachings of the Buddha. This kingdom ended up following the Buddha's example of equality, as people from all races, ethnicities, sexual orientations, religious preferences, and class backgrounds were united under one banner of mindfulness and compassion. That kingdom was known as Shambhala.

Shambhala is a story that illustrates that peace is possible if we can learn to overcome our internal warfare and love more fully. Chögyam Trungpa Rinpoche has pointed out, "Meditation practice is regarded as a good and in fact excellent way to overcome warfare in the world: our own warfare as well as greater warfare."[17] World peace starts with examining our own mind through meditation and contemplation. This is not necessarily a Buddhist thing; meditation is practiced in many traditions. But if you want world peace, you need to overcome your internal warfare before looking to love yourself and others.

The nice thing is that we have a choice, in every moment, to be kind or be a jerk. There is a Native American story of an elderly man who taught his grandson about peace. He told his grandson that he felt that there were two wolves that lived within his heart. One was fueled by anger and aggression, the other by kindness. The two wolves were constantly at war with each other for his heart. His grandson asked who would ultimately win in such a fight. The grandfather answered, "The one that wins will be the one I choose to feed."

Which wolf are you feeding on a day-by-day basis? The wolf that keeps you habituated to the speed and aggression of today's society? Or the wolf that goes against the stream of society and demands that we practice kindness in all of our endeavors? Which would you like to feed? Meditation can help you with that.

Whatever comes up in your life, you can be kind. You can dance with whatever life presents you, whether it is joyful or painful, and respond with gentleness. Pema Chödrön has said, "We can dance with life when it's a wild party completely out of control, and we can dance with life when it's as tender as a lover. We work with whatever we have, with whoever we are, right now."[18] No matter what comes up, we can work with it. We can expand our hearts to accommodate anything. If you want to create world peace, you must start there. You must start with kindness. I cannot guarantee that you will single-handedly save the world, but if you can live a life based on kindness, you will certainly move it in the right direction.

5 / WORK LIKE A BUDDHA

Your work is to discover your work and then with all of your heart to give yourself to it.

—*Siddhartha Gautama*

So many of us get up, rush through our morning routine and commute, and then spend the majority of our waking hours at work. At the end of our shifts we rush home to squeeze as much pleasure out of the little amount of free time we have. That sounds like a pretty wasteful way to live our life, living for the weekend.

Thankfully, Buddhism shows us that we have an alternative path. If you are able to slow down and be present with your life, you can enjoy it fully. You can take pleasure in the warmth of your morning shower or the mariachi band on your subway ride to and from work, and most important, you can enjoy every moment you are engaged in your chosen profession, simply through applying mindfulness. You could be a tattoo artist, an executive at a media agency, a doctor, or a clerk at a convenience store, but if you are able to apply mindfulness and compassion to your work, then you will be able to find contentment during your nine to five. With the right perspective you can transform your office into a meditation hall.

Choosing a Career Path

> I've found that in college, grad school, and early career life, very little emphasis is put on how a career path fits an individual; rather, the emphasis is on how the individual should strive to change in a way that adapts to the career path he or she has (arbitrarily) selected. What should one really know about oneself while planning a career path? What kinds of reflection might facilitate this level of self-knowledge?

While traveling for my book tour, I had the rare opportunity to go back to college. In fact, I went back to a few dozen of them. Some felt very similar to my alma mater, Wesleyan University, and others felt very different. The common thread among all of these experiences is that I met with a lot of young people, and none of them knew how to approach the task of determining their career path.

I always had the idea while growing up that college and grad school were supposed to prepare you for your chosen profession. If you did not know what you wanted to be when you grew up by the time you entered college, you certainly would by the time you left it. That did not prove to be the case for me, and I know I am no exception.

As I talked about this scary transition to the work world with so many students and college graduates, it became clear that the big question for these individuals would not be *what* do I want to *do* when I grow up but *who* do I want to *be*? Some young people thought they knew exactly what they wanted to do, which post they wanted in a certain field, or what company they would ideally work for upon leaving the confines of school. Other people had no sense whatsoever and were willing to move to a new town or city and just explore what came up. The question that opens this chapter points to my experience of these individuals, in that for both people with direction and those without, the students were looking to find a career that they could mold themselves to as opposed to getting to know themselves first.

I came to the conclusion around this time that the age-old notion that we have something that we are finally doing as a "grown-up" is a fallacy. None of us think we are grown-up. When you are in your teenage years, you think that when you're in your midtwenties and out on your own you will have it all figured out. Then when you hit that point, you see people in their thirties and say, "Well, they finally know what they're doing; I can't wait until I'm there." Then when you are in your thirties, you look toward your forties, knowing that surely by then you will be able to claim that "grown-up" status of having your shit completely together.

At some point we have to realize that we are constantly changing, adapting human beings. There is no final end point where we are done growing up. Benjamin Franklin once famously declared, "When you're finished changing, you're finished." The only escape from change and this continual path of growing up is death. That is when we are done changing.

I throw out the D word not to scare anyone but to note that we have two ways we can live our lives in relating to our careers. You can stumble out into the world, take the first job offered that sounds mildly appealing, and bounce between positions and companies in that field until something better comes along. Alternatively, you can determine who you want to be and infuse your entire career path with the qualities you want to cultivate. If you are able to do that, regardless of where you are on your work journey, you have begun to treat it as a practice opportunity. This latter way of relating to your career path will likely bring you more clarity about what you ought to do for work and also make your time here on earth more fulfilling.

I have come to realize that this question of who we want to be, as opposed to what we want to do, may be something we should all contemplate, regardless of how old we are or where we are in our career path. The notion of determining who we want to be is rooted in the Buddhist teachings on discernment. Earlier we talked about the natural process on the meditation cushion, where the same sorts of story lines and emotional content come up over and over again. Our path is to continually come back to the breath, our anchor in the present moment. As we rise from the meditation cushion, we start to have a better sense of our mind and how these story lines and emotional hooks play out in our lives. We start to discern which aspects of our lives we want to cultivate and which we want to reject.

Through the practice of meditation, you might figure out certain things about yourself. You might see that when you volunteer at a certain place, you feel great joy. When you drink too much, you lose a day to your hangover. When you spend time with one sort of friend, you feel that you are being supported and have good conversations. When you spend time with a different group of friends, you end up bad-mouthing others and feel conflicted about your status within the group. The more present you are in your day-to-day life, the more you are able to see skillfully which activities and people you ought to spend more time on and which you should gently cut out.

You can apply this same process to determining how you want to approach your career path. Perhaps you have discerned, on and off the meditation cushion, that you want to live a life with less stress or based on kindness or offering compassion to everyone you meet. If you can take these aspects of your discernment and make them priorities in your life, you will have a greater chance of living a life with meaning. You can say "I want to be a calm person" or "I want to be a kind person" or "I want to be the sort of person who gives back every chance I get."

What I would recommend is that once you have determined the quality or qualities you want to have as a core tenet of your life, you write this statement out. You can print it on nice paper and frame it or write it out in calligraphy or paint it, but make it something that you will actually want to look at regularly. Then post it somewhere that you will see it, either at work or at home.

Take this key phrase you have developed as a regular point of contemplation. When you wake up in the morning, reflect on that aspiration. Before you go to bed at night, think about how much of your time that day you were able to spend fulfilling your aspiration. Don't get too judgmental here; just acknowledge what happened in your day and celebrate whatever small victories might present themselves. If you are trying to be a kind person and you refrained from snapping at that jerk who stepped on your foot in your morning commute, that's not bad! Be gentle when analyzing how you're doing regarding living in line with your intention.

The more time you spend contemplating this basic quality you want to cultivate, the more you bring it into reality in your daily life. You are gradually turning your mind to kindness or compassion or any other aspect that you want to bring forth more in your existence. That is self-knowledge. The more you know about yourself, the more you will be able to discern which jobs will allow you to develop those qualities you want to cultivate. You can bring your discernment to choosing professions that are suited to who you want to be as opposed to what you want to do. To that end, as part of my own work I founded an institute to help people with this transition from spending their hours working solely for a steady paycheck to positioning themselves as authentic leaders, engaging employment they find meaningful (more on that on my Web site at www.lodrorinzler.com).

The beauty of this process is that you can collect garbage for a living or run a hedge fund. If you know yourself well and continue to reflect on the qualities you want to cultivate in your life, you will feel contentment. You are determining who you want to be and what qualities you want to cultivate and not letting your specific job or title or company define you. You are doing what you want to be doing. You are being the you you want to be. While it is great to start this contemplation practice early on, it is still going to be a lifelong journey.

Presenting Yourself at an Interview

I'm currently looking for a job and interviewing a lot. I don't really feel confident in these interviews. I want to be confident and show my best aspects, but I don't know how.

I am reminded of a commercial for a new Google product. In it a man is waiting in an office, clearly preparing for an important meeting or interview. He is practicing how to introduce himself. Then he spots a picture of a castle on the wall, stands up, and uses this Google feature to determine which castle it is. When the person he is meeting walks in, he casually turns around and says, "Have you ever been to this castle?" and reveals all of his newly discovered knowledge about it.

So many of us are like this fictional worker, nervous about our ability and wanting to please the person with whom we are interviewing. We want to pretend to know the person, so we try to force familiarity, and we want the person to like us, so we present only the best parts of who we are. This level of trickery flies in the face of living an authentic life.

When you sit down with someone for a job interview, don't try to present yourself as anything other than yourself. Don't pretend to know the interviewer but try to get to know her or him in an open and genuine manner. In my own experience, if I sat down with someone and talked about certain aspects of my job experience, trying to fit my own work into something relevant to the interviewer while downplaying other aspects of what I have done and who I am . . . well, those interviews have never have gone well. Similarly, if I have made assumptions about the interviewer, their intention for doing their job, or what their work looked like, I was in for trouble.

However, if I sat down and presented all of who I am, including my Buddhist background, I found that interviewers were intrigued. In the job-interview process, it is somewhat unusual for someone to come in and just lay all of his or her cards down on the table, including both the aces and the two of spades. It is refreshing to meet someone and immediately enter into an authentic relationship with the person. When you do that you offer an invitation to the person interviewing you to reciprocate and let you know his or her own experience of the position being discussed.

I have been on the other side of that table and have had other people come in and try to convince me that they are the right person for a job. There have been occasions when, halfway through an interview, I find out that the interviewer is hiding something. That something is a part of who the person is and is worth discussing, be it the person's having taken time off from work to care for a young child or having been fired at some time but being embarrassed and thinking I would be unsympathetic. It is never helpful to walk in and think that the person you are meeting with would not want to know who you are. That would be calling the person's own basic goodness into question. You are simultaneously doubting that you can be hired based on who you are and doubting the other person's ability to keep an open mind.

I have found that no level of insight into the other person and no vast knowledge of the art hanging in a room will compare to presenting yourself authentically. If you have faith in your own ability, present that. That is something people want to see. If you doubt yourself and worry that you're not the right person for the job, that is something your interviewer will remember in a negative light.

Not too long ago I sat down for an interview at the White House. I wasn't even sure I was interested in a job in the president's administration, but you don't really say no to an interview at the White House. Because I was unsure about how badly I wanted the job, I took some time to analyze my motivation for being there. I realized that I was meeting about a job that was in line with who I want to be as opposed to solely relating to what I want to do. In this case, I knew I wanted to be of benefit to others, and working in this capacity seemed like a way I could do that. Once I was clear about my own motivation, the interview flowed seamlessly because I was able to present more of who I am rather than just what I do.

When you go on a job interview, present all of who you are and trust that that is okay. Show who you are, not what you do. Who you are is fascinating and memorable. An interviewer may see dozens of people who have five-plus years of management experience, but she or he will never see another you again. Use that to your advantage.

Overcoming Office Gossip and Slander

> I've worked with basically the same group of people in my office for about four years—to the point where we're almost like family. The problem is that this group has become so negative that I can hardly stand it. Everyone we work with outside our office, every client—and every current event from elections to Lindsay Lohan's behavior—is spoken about sarcastically and critically in a way that helps no one and that has made the atmosphere in the office toxic. I can't really identify how this process began, but I know that I'm as much a part of it as any of my colleagues are—and I don't know the best way to change the climate. I feel that if I don't respond to all the negative talk in kind, I'll be taken to be acting holier-than-thou and will likely get ostracized, and I don't think it would change anything. I'm at a loss for how to change things. Any ideas?

There are so many things that can make an office environment toxic, but mindless speech seems to be chief among them. You might show up at a new job and feel welcomed. Everyone is so friendly. Then over lunch one day someone drops some juicy gossip about your latest client. You're intrigued and share it with your other coworker in the hopes of hearing more. Before you know it you are entrenched in verbal warfare—you are shooting off rumors and barbs about others and worrying that they might be attacking you in the same way behind your back.

Mindless speech is an easy way to cause a great deal of harm. Knowing that you are not interested in doing that, I would recommend following the Buddha's teachings on what are known as the four gates of speech, which follow.

1. Is What You Are Saying True?

Analyzing the first gate may prevent you from going forward on your verbal attack. If you are about to say something (positive or negative) that you are not 100 percent certain is true, don't say it. You don't really know what is going on in Lindsay Lohan's life; you weren't there for her most recent arrest or the incident that preceded it. There is no need to comment on things you don't know about. If you hit this gate and are not confident that whatever you have to say is true, then don't say anything at all.

2. Is What I Am Saying Necessary?

The second gate is a bit more subtle, and it's harder to distinguish whether you ought to pass through it. It is natural to want to bullshit a little bit when you are at work or when you're in an uncomfortable situation. You might boast about an upcoming project or let slip that two people in accounting are sleeping together or just ask a lot of inane questions. If you constantly come back to the idea of saying only what is necessary, you will come off as truly genuine. People respect genuine. They are magnetized by it. If you can pass through this gate on a regular basis, then you will begin changing the office environment, as more and more people want to interact with the guy or gal that won't bullshit them.

3. Is What I Am Saying Kind?

The third gate you have to pass through before speaking is one based on gentleness and compassion. Even if something is true and it is necessary to talk about it, that doesn't mean it's going to be kind. You can contemplate, "Will saying this create hurt or harm?" If you believe it will be helpful to other people, say your piece. If it will only create destruction without any positive outcome, hold your tongue. The fourteenth-century meditation master Ngulchu Thogme Zangpo said,

> Harsh words disturb the minds of others
> And compromise a Bodhisattva's right conduct.
> Therefore, to give up harsh and unpleasant speech
> Is the practice of a Bodhisattva.

Avoid harsh words so as not to compromise your conduct. We should strive to be kind in all things but particularly in our speech.

4. Is It the Right Time?

The final gate is like a well-told joke: it's all about timing. When you sit down with a coworker and you want to debrief the person on one of your outside clients, there may be some things that are worth saying during this initial conversation and others that you may need to sit on. Just because you're excited to tell your coworker something doesn't mean that it's the time to dive into murky waters. This gate may be based on your coworker's attention span, what else he or she might have going on that day, or just making sure you know the full picture of a situation before communicating it to another.

Because I'm in a listy mood, I'm going to throw out a few

more communication pointers. These are the six points of mindful speech as articulated by Chögyam Trungpa Rinpoche:

1. Speak slowly
2. Enunciate clearly
3. Listen to yourself
4. Listen to others
5. Regard silence as a part of speech
6. Speak concisely

When you are ready to communicate something, try to speak in a way that will allow other people to hear you. That means speaking slowly and enunciating well. That also includes practicing deep listening techniques, where you are able both to hear what you are saying and to listen to the person with whom you are speaking. In the course of your conversation with someone, do not be afraid to let there be a lot of space. Space, in this speedy world, is always a good thing.

Along those lines, silence can speak volumes, particularly when someone is trying to engage you in negative conversation. The final pointer here is that whether you are having a positive or a negative conversation, be concise. Don't overstate your case; just use the words that are necessary. Employing these six points of mindful speech ensures good communication and that you are not causing harm in your speech, in or out of the office.

It is easy to fall into the habitual pattern of a given environment, be it an office, a family, or a group of friends. However, if you want to shift the dynamic in a positive way, work with the four gates of speech and six points of mindful speech. These simple guidelines shift your own speech and allow others the opportunity to meet you in that new form of communication.

You may initially fear creating this change in your environment, but long-term, people will be delighted that you offer so much thoughtfulness and authenticity in your communication. It may take time, but your coworkers will likely respond in kind, and then you will have turned the tide of speech so that your office is based on kindness again.

Do It for the Money or for the Meaning?

> I'm graduating this month and have two good job leads. One is at an environmental nonprofit, but the pay is horrible. I have always wanted my work to do some good in the world, though. The other is at a global company that doesn't seem to me to benefit anyone, but the pay is awesome. I'm mired in debt and could really use the money. What does Buddhism say about life balance (and often trade-off) and working for money? Is this the wrong motivation?

I certainly understand the desire to take a secure job where you have a good salary. I can't imagine anyone's outright faulting you for that desire. You could group that sort of decision under the heading of taking care of yourself. Furthermore, I think it's brave for people interested in mindfulness and compassion to bring those aspects of themselves to work in major corporate settings. In that sort of environment, we are constantly being tested in our ability to keep an open heart when confronted with ruthless office politics, gossip, and manipulation.

Now, I am not someone who frequents the gym, but my understanding is that when you work out, you are supposed to go a little bit above and beyond your comfort zone, and that is when the muscle begins to grow. The same can be said for your heart. If you can remain openhearted above and beyond your usual comfort level, you are stretching your compassion muscle and growing as a person. You are giving yourself a compassion workout, which leads to your growing as a person.

For example, I think it's incorrect to say that working as an analyst at a major corporation would benefit no one. You could engage your workplace as a meditation space and learn to work with the range of emotions you encounter on the spot. That could be an excellent practice for you. Also, not to get too Gandhi on you, but being openhearted in the workplace (any workplace) demonstrates a little bit of that change many of us would like to see take place in major corporations.

Obviously, I cannot make this sort of decision for anyone; it is up to each person to make this choice between pay and life-style. However, I do want to touch on right livelihood. As part of the Eightfold Path, the Buddha taught that we should not pursue work that harms ourselves or others. If you are offered an analyst position you may feel that job would harm others. Maybe you would be doing research in support of liberal gun laws and believe in your heart that you would be only a few steps away from peddling firearms to children.

I'm not sure which brand of poison the company you are considering working for sells, but if you don't agree with the mission statement of an organization, you will probably not feel comfortable working there. In fact, doing something you do not feel good about will drain your own life energy, regardless of how much money you are putting in the bank. As the eighth-century Buddhist scholar Shantideva said,

Some evil and lustful people
Wear themselves out by working all day
And when they return home (in the evening)
Their exhausted bodies lie prostrate like corpses.[1]

It is funny how a text written thirteen hundred years ago can still sound familiar today. Granted, the language is a bit strong (I'm not going to call you, dear reader, evil or lustful), but the basic idea behind this verse remains relevant. How many of us come home after a long day of work, flop down on our couch, and flick on the television, spending the rest of the evening prostrate like a corpse?

We have a choice: we can live in such a way that our work brings us energy, or we can live in a way in which it drains our energy. The distinction lies in whether you engage work that you feel is significant. A recent study showed that the most important thing to members of the Millennial Generation when they looked for work was that the job would be meaningful. This quality outranked both high pay and sense of accomplishment.

If you were offered a job that paid well and another that would allow you to help others, you might want to ask yourself, "What would feel meaningful to me?" Ideally, you could find a job that would be meaningful, allow you to cultivate qualities you want in yourself, and also pay well. However, if you are like the person who asked the question for this section and your primary motivation is to do some good in this world, then you ought to let that notion inform your decision.

When faced with major life decisions, it might be helpful to recall that our old friend Death is never too far away. We don't know when he will come visit—only that he will come. We could live a good ninety-five years or get hit by a bus tomorrow. Trust me; I know. I've been hit by a bus. I offer this tangent not as a downer but as a reminder that we ought to make the most of this life and appreciate the time we have. We need to live all of our life with intent, and that most definitely includes the long hours we log at the office.

When you are lying on your deathbed, I doubt that you will cry out, "I wish I'd watched more TV!" or "If only I had had nicer clothes!" The author Bronnie Ware worked in palliative care for a number of years. Her book, *The Top Five Regrets of the Dying*, lists the five main misgivings of the individuals she encountered during her years of serving as a nurse. Surprisingly, the number one regret was "I wish I'd had the courage to live a life true to myself, not the life others expected of me."

It might be worth reflecting on this regret when making significant decisions on your career path. Years from now will you have lived a life true to yourself? Will you be surrounded by the people you have helped along the way? Will they remind you of the significant accomplishments that made a difference in the lives of others? While you may be tempted to make short-term decisions based on immediate needs or desires, make sure you take a long-term view and engage work that you find meaningful, regardless of the paycheck.

You've Got (Mindful) Mail!

I am on my computer all day long for work, mainly responding to e-mails. Is there any Buddhist view on how to spend time on e-mail mindfully?

Obviously, at the time of the Buddha, e-mail did not exist. However, he did teach extensively about mindfulness. If you cannot make something as basic as e-mailing a colleague a part of your meditation application, then you likely won't be able to apply your practice in more quick-paced, intense conflicts. So perhaps we can think through a number of ways to make this everyday activity a true spiritual practice.

Allow me to posit ten steps as a method for beginning your e-mail meditation training:

1. When you receive an e-mail, *read the whole message first*. Don't leap into fixed mind, thinking you know what the other person is going to say. Take a fresh-start approach to this process and be thorough in your reading. Sometimes tone is hard to perceive in e-mail form, so take the time to read the whole thing, twice if needed.

Let the words sink in. If there is feedback or news in the e-mail, notice what it brings up. Don't start composing your response as you read the e-mail; just see what emotional and mental reactions come up. You don't have to cling to those reactions. Relax with whatever arises.

2. Unless it's something superspecific, such as "Can you remind me what time we're meeting?" *give it some space and time*. If it is superspecific, then maybe you can go ahead and write a simple, straightforward answer. For example:

Hi Oliver,
We're meeting at 5 pm.
See you then!

Best,
Nancy

If the e-mail is about something other than asking what time an event is going to happen or asking you to send over a document for review, don't feel that you need to respond simply to get the e-mail out of your in-box. I'm as much a fan as getting to an empty in-box as anyone but not at the expense of sloppy communication.

I employ a simple method for nonurgent e-mails that I know will require some thought: I sort them into a specific folder entitled Open. These open-issue e-mails are still on my mind, but I might read them a few times before responding, so I want to provide a space for them and the mental energy I've committed to them. The Open file gives them a home where they're not in my face but are still on my mind.

3. In general, *respond when you are able* to do so properly. Figure out when you can give the other person your full attention. You can apply your sense of discernment to this task, acknowledging which e-mails will take up your mental energy and waiting until you can attend to them properly while responding right away to those e-mails that require a little energy from you.

4. *Greetings and signatures are important.* When I was starting my first job, the person who previously held my post warned me about how to work with a particularly difficult individual. He had very simple advice for me. "When e-mailing, always

put in a clear greeting and signature," he said, "because people respect elegance." It's true. Notice how you feel when you get e-mails that don't even acknowledge your name or that make a demand without any sense of gratitude or personalization.

The next time you get such an e-mail, reread it, mentally inserting a "Dear So-and-So" at the beginning and a "Thank you so much" signature at the end. Would you be more willing to respect the person who sends an e-mail like that and to reply to it ahead of one from a person who just makes demands without pleasantries? While this may seem like it's not strictly Buddhist, we know that the Buddha taught extensively on kindness and mindful speech; this seems like a simple way to move in that direction.

5. When you sit down to respond to an e-mail, *reread what the sender said*. See if you notice things that were not obvious in your first reading. Maintain a vast mind in order to get an overall feel for what the person is expressing, but allow yourself the opportunity to get specific with what he or she is asking of you.

6. Personally, when responding to long e-mails, I like to *go line by line* through what the other person said so I make sure I am not missing a vital point. All too often it is easy to type a rapid response to someone and feel good about it until you get something back five minutes later asking, "And what did you think of the final point? You know, the one I said I really needed your opinion on?" When that happens, you feel like a bit of an idiot. Slow down and be present enough to listen fully to everything the other person is saying.

7. As you work on your e-mail, take a moment to *reflect on the four gates of speech and the six points of mindful speech*, as detailed earlier in this chapter. It might be helpful to print them out and have them on your desk or in your work environment so that they serve as regular reminders for your speech, both verbal and electronic.

8. Before you click send, *reread what you wrote*. Does it conform to what you want to say? Are you clear? Is it concise? Does it show that you actually listened to the other person?

9. If so, *click send.*

10. Then *rest your mind* for a few moments before moving on to the next task. Allow yourself that moment of completion and transition.

While this may sound like a lot of work, particularly if you get a hundred or more e-mails a day (I've been there), you may find that taking the space to communicate well will save you time in the long run. If you take the time to apply mindfulness to this everyday task and address people clearly by e-mail, you may find that you do not have to have as much back-and-forth with them to clarify what each of you meant.

Try these ten steps for mindful e-mail communication, even if just for one difficult e-mail a day, and see if you feel refreshed or drained afterward. If these ten steps work for you and you are able to be present for this basic task, wonderful. If not, try just the last step after each e-mail over the course of an hour. Just resting your mind for a moment between messages can help cut through speed and bring mindfulness to your e-mailing, making the ordinary extraordinary.

THE BULLY BOSS

I am working as a researcher for a pharmaceutical company, and I am being severely bullied by my boss. He steals credit from me, tells lies about me to coworkers, and belittles me in front of clients. Since my immigration status is tied to this employer for now, I have to stick it out for probably another six months. Honestly, I do harbor revenge fantasies for all the psychological stress I have to endure right now. I can't wait for the day when I am free and can tell him what a dirty little jerk he is. In rare moments I do feel compassion for him, since he is a tormented soul and I know he must suffer greatly to be so abusive to other people. How would you recommend I handle this situation?

So many of us have been placed in a situation where our boss acts in ways that are far from ideal. Just the other night I was at dinner with my friend Kate. She works as a sommelier at one of the best restaurants in the New York City area and has, in her own words, her dream job. The only thing that transforms that dream into a sometimes nightmare is her boss. "In many ways, I think I'm an ideal employee," Kate said. "I'm bright, I'm cheerful, I always do what is asked of me, and I enjoy it, so I never complain." It was painful to watch the energy of this radiant woman being gradually drained, day after day, by a boss who did many of the things mentioned in the letter above.

Many of us have at one point or another felt that our hard work has not been acknowledged or that we've taken blame when it was not due, or someone has agreed to do something at work and then immediately done the opposite, or we've been hurt by slanderous speech. Having all of the above coming from one person (and on a consistent basis) is a tough position to be in.

One set of Shambhala Buddhist teachings I've always found helpful in workplace drama is known as the Six Ways of Ruling, which teach us to face aggression with compassion. As the Tibetan Buddhist teacher Tulku Urgyen Rinpoche used to tell his students, "Being aggressive, you can accomplish some things, but with gentleness, you can accomplish all things." We can all try to accomplish our goals with these six principles in mind.

1. Benevolent

The first step is trying to remain open and accommodating by not taking things too personally. This is tough, I know. However, you might notice that your boss torments people other than yourself. A lot of times when someone in the workplace is stressed, the person does not know how to relax and ends up taking it out on others. Giving this person's aggression patience and space can be an incredible act of compassion.

Imagine an angry bull. If put in a small pen, an angry bull will continue to buck around, unable to release his tension. However, if you take that animal and put it in an open field, he will run around until he tires himself out. The same can be said of someone's aggression. If you can remain *benevolent* (the first of the six ways of ruling), then you have a shot at weathering this thing. Perhaps the image of the angry bull might inspire a sense of humor in you. Keeping a sense of humor and not taking things personally are ways of keeping an open mind in the midst of aggression. So step one: practice benevolence by being patient and spacious.

2. True

This is not to say that you should lie down like a doormat when your boss is a jerk. At times you may need to say something to your boss in order to set the record straight. When you do need to do that, it's important to choose your words carefully. Bringing mindfulness into your speech, you can be *true* to your own wisdom while empowering your words with a sense of weight.

Being true in this sense is not simply being diplomatic but is actually connecting with your heart. *Bodhicitta* serves as the generator of your wisdom. Remaining true to yourself while confronting tough issues inspires natural confidence. So if you find yourself being bullied, say something and say it from your heart, not from a point of politics or protocol.

3. Genuine

This takes us into the third way of ruling, being *genuine*. It sounds pretty straightforward (don't be fake), but it's a bit more complex. The idea of being genuine is that when you have a point to make, you ground it in logic. As Sakyong Mipham Rinpoche has said, "It is not even our genuineness particularly.

It is just genuine, a star in the sky that everyone can see. We all recognize the truth."[2] In other words, if you are at work and clearly see that something needs to be done, then disregard previous animosity and attempt to guide your boss toward that goal with logic. It's not about one of you being right and the other wrong but attempting to show a clear course of action.

If you continue to remain gentle in the face of aggression, it can have a transformative effect on not only your employer but your whole office situation. As the Sakyong wrote in his book *Ruling Your World*, "Gentleness is always the best whip, one that everyone respects, because it is devoted to the welfare of others."[3] We garner respect from others because they come to learn that our actions are rooted in our own wisdom and the practicalities of the situation at hand.

4. Fearless

Along those lines, when it is time for us to make a decision at work, we need to be *fearless*. Whether you are a researcher, a sommelier, a surgeon, or a painter, I am guessing that when you are at work, you think through quite carefully whatever actions need to be taken. Thus, when it is time to actually do something, act fearlessly. If you are reticent about how you feel things ought to be done, that takes the wind out of the sails of an entire project. Fear can be contagious, so have faith in yourself and your basic goodness.

5. Artful

The fifth way of ruling is being *artful*. Ruling your work situation is an art, not a science. You can set your day up skillfully to maximize your time and spend it with coworkers with whom you know you can accomplish a great deal. Taking some time to review the work environment, you can ask yourself, "What is the most appropriate time to pitch a new idea?" Before calling out your boss on something you feel negative about, ask,

"How will this help?" I am not saying sit back and let the boss be mean to you, but I am suggesting you keep an open mind about the circumstances around you. Consideration for others is at the root of being artful. With consideration we open up a space for others to discover their own wisdom.

6. Rejoicing

Giving yourself and others space is worthy of *rejoicing*, the sixth way of ruling. It is so hard not to respond to aggression with aggression, not to want to change someone who is causing you suffering. Yet you know in your heart that the only thing you can change is your own actions. Looking upon your workplace with mindfulness, space, and compassion is a practice—a legitimate practice, just like what you do on the meditation cushion. When you look at your life in this way, you may find that you are happier in your skin. You feel comfortable because you are being true to yourself in the midst of great obstacles. We should celebrate that.

The Sakyong has said that when we employ the six ways of ruling, "we no longer believe that we can get what we want with negativity. We're using different strategies. We understand how power flows: by resting in a big mind, we can conquer small mind."[4] In Kate's case, her boss found out that he couldn't get what he wanted with negativity and ended up having to leave this dream job of a restaurant; he self-destructed and is no longer her boss. You may not be as fortunate, so I wish you luck conquering small mind through employing the six ways of ruling.

WE ARE ALL IN CUSTOMER SERVICE

How do you coexist with jerks at work?

I'm going to go out on a limb with this question and say that the most straightforward way to get along with people at the office is to start by not calling them jerks. When you solidify another person, be it your lover, your mother, or your coworker, with a set title such as "my everything" or "my rock" or "that jerk," you are limiting your perspective of who the person is. As Michael Carroll, author of *Fearless at Work*, has said, "Too often we can mistake our opinions for facts."[5] When you transform your opinions into facts, you are bound for conflict.

At one point, in a somewhat private meeting, Sakyong Mipham Rinpoche told me, "Our job is to relate with people." I have continued to contemplate that idea in the months that have followed. If you go to work with this phrase on your mind, you can interact with everyone there with the mentality that your job is not just "sales clerk" or "educator" or "social worker" but that you are, in essence, in customer service.

We are all in customer service. I believe the Sakyong is right: our whole job is to relate with people. It doesn't matter if you are interacting with only a handful of clients in person in a given day. In the modern workplace we are constantly in touch with dozens to hundreds of people through e-mail and phone calls. Our job is not to relate just with clients, though; we have to treat our coworkers with the same respect we would our most promising lead. Even if your coworkers act in a confused manner and come off as jerks, your job is to relate to them as fully and openheartedly as you can. That is your job.

While he was not in customer service and did not work in the modern workplace, Shantideva knew this basic principle quite well. He said,

> Enslaving others, forcing them to serve me,
> I will come to know the state of servitude.
> But if I labor for the good of others,
> Mastery and leadership will come to me.[6]

If you go to work with the idea that you are going to treat your jerk-like coworkers as second-class citizens, trying to manipulate them to get what you want from them, you are missing the point. That is no way to solve employee conflicts. Instead, you can labor on their behalf, being as helpful to them as you can stomach. This shift in view, in not meeting jerk-like energy with jerk-life energy, smashes preconceived notions of your workplace environment like the Incredible Hulk in an IKEA (everyone gets angry at IKEA).

If you can break away from interacting with your coworkers on a habitual level, you may find that they come to respect you over time. As Shantideva points out, if someone labors solely for your own good, you tend to want to help out that person in turn. You end up becoming a leader worth honoring in your workplace, which is something that is much needed in today's work environment.

Instead of meeting your jerk coworkers in a tit-for-tat relationship, I encourage you to try understanding more about them. That is a surefire way to become a better leader, someone your coworkers will admire. Thich Nhat Hanh once wrote, "Understanding is the essence of love. If you cannot understand, you cannot love."[7] I am not saying you should fall in love with your coworkers in a romantic sense, but I'm not opposed to your falling in love with them from a less conventional point of view.

True love, in a Buddhist context, is being willing to accept everyone you encounter without reservation. It is appreciating people for who they are as opposed to who you want them to be. That includes your coworkers. You should most definitely try to understand who they are and, as a result, learn to love them just as you would your parents or other beings who have shown you unbelievable kindness.

There is a children's story I enjoy very much that feels relevant to this discussion: A long time ago in China, a monk climbed up a tree. He sat there meditating, largely undisturbed by the outside world, sometimes imparting thoughtful words to people passing by. He became known as Birdsnest for his high roosting place.

At one point a local ruler heard of this wise man and set out to meet him. After a long and arduous trek, he found Birdsnest's tree. He shouted up at the monk, telling him that he had a very important question to ask of him. He waited for Birdsnest to reply, but no response came. He continued anyway: "This is my question. Tell me, Birdsnest, what is it that all the wise ones have taught? Can you tell me the most important thing the Buddha ever said?" He waited again, for a very long time.

Finally, Birdsnest called down. He said, "Don't do bad things. Always do good things. That's what all the buddhas taught." The local ruler became annoyed at this monk, who was clearly downplaying the power of the Buddha's teachings. He yelled back, "That's your advice? I knew that when I was three years old, monk!" Birdsnest looked down at him, his compassion radiating out. "Yes, the three-year-old knows it," he said, "but the eighty-year-old still finds it very difficult to do!"

The simplest way to coexist with your coworkers is to get to know them well, learn to love them, and do only good things for them. Even if you think they are jerks now, you can revisit your three-year-old training and remember to avoid harming them and to help them, and then see if your view of them changes over time. See if the way they react and interact with you changes. If you are truly kind to them, taking their happiness as your job, then you will be the best customer service representative ever born. You can take these jerks as your job and transform your workplace with the potency of kindness.

To Quit or Not To Quit

I'm trying to decide whether I want to quit my job or not. It's a tough market right now. At the same time, I feel that I'm just going through the motions at work, that maybe it's not right livelihood, and I don't really care about what we're selling. Help!

The good news for anyone contemplating quitting her or his job and eyeing the economy skeptically is that you're not alone.

So many of us are raised with the belief that when we grow up, we can be anything we want to be. Yet few of us are really sure what that should look like. If you are lucky enough to have figured that out, you might still struggle when faced with the limited options that come with the current economic climate.

As I mentioned before, the Buddha laid out right livelihood as part of the Eightfold Path to enlightenment. These teachings serve as a guide that can allow us to discern how to create a positive force for change while we're engaged in our nine to five. In brief, it refers to not causing harm, by being employed in a legal and peaceful way. Given that laws change from culture to culture and over time and that the word *peaceful* is a highly subjective term, we have to realize that these teachings are entirely up to interpretation. To get traditional for a moment, there are five specific aspects to right livelihood:

1. You can't deal in living beings. This includes not going into prostitution, raising animals for slaughter, being involved in slavery, or doing any of your other usual Sunday-afternoon activities (kidding).

2. You can't make money selling weapons. If you sell guns or work in foreign-arms deals, that means you.

3. You can't make money selling poison. In other words, you can't profit off any life-taking device. This is not just human poison, of course, but even products such as roach spray.

4. You can't make money selling intoxicants. No selling drugs or alcohol.

5. You can't make money selling meat. That means you, guy on my corner selling turkey sandwiches out of a bodega.

As you begin to peruse the list, it may strike you as very sensible. It sounds like it's a good idea not to be a pimp or a pig butcher. You didn't want to do that anyway. However, if you continue along this list, you see that under a strict interpretation of these teachings, you can't do any number of things. You were breaking from the teachings that summer you worked at Subway because you were profiting from selling meat. That part-time job you wanted to take bartending so you can help make ends meet? A break from the teachings. Even the person coming around the neighborhood selling cooking knives could, under a strict reading, be considered someone selling weapons.

The point of the Buddha's teachings is not to get everything "right" from a conventional point of view. The point of the teachings is to wake up to your own mind and heart in a true form. It is to discover what "right" means to you. Through the practice of meditation, you are offered a glimpse of your own innate wisdom. The more you can tune in to that wisdom, the more you can allow it to guide you to spend your time in ways that you feel are in line with what you ought to be doing with this life. You have to engage in your own process of thorough self-examination in order to discern what livelihood feels right to you.

Please note that I'm making a pretty large distinction here: being bored at work is different from feeling that what you are doing is not in tune with your own noble intentions. If you are feeling the latter, I think you might have found the personal grounds on which to quit. Even if you have a good paycheck or a lot of vacation time, you will likely not be happy if you are engaged in a full-time job that is not "right" for your own heart. If you are feeling the former, though, perhaps I can offer a very different recommendation.

I believe that so many of us are bored at work because we are not willing or able to bring our full selves to the tasks at hand. Either we are being underutilized or we feel that we are not being assigned to the projects that best fit our skill set or we think that our particular knowledge base is not being called upon. When that happens, we check out. Our habitual instinct is to retract our full level of attention from our work and operate with the bare minimum required of us.

I remember meeting with my friend Hylke once and discussing some part-time work I was engaged in. I shared the sentiment expressed in this question, one of not feeling sure whether the company I was working for was the right fit for me. His advice was phenomenal. Hylke suggested that I just notice when I felt a reluctance to perform fully for the company and drop that reluctance like a meditator drops a particularly strong thought. Then just come back to the present.

Within the present moment there is always the potential for a fresh start. Within the present moment there is no such thing as boredom. There is only possibility. So if you are bored, drop the boredom like a hot coal and just come back to the reality of your situation as it is. See if you can find contentment in this very moment.

If you are engaged in work that you find does not fall under the umbrella of your understanding of right livelihood, then you should probably leave it. Try not to get lost in fear-based thinking about the job market and high unemployment rates: have faith in your basic goodness, present yourself authentically in all endeavors, and strive to find a job that is truly in line with your own noble heart.

BEING AUTHENTIC AT YOUR SHITTY JOB

How do I leave behind the feeling of being trapped in my job and the resentment it causes? I want to be authentic at work.

You never leave feelings behind, in my experience. You can go through a horrible breakup, think you're over your ex, then months later hear about the ex dating another person and experience all of those same painful feelings anew. Emotions come and go, like the waves of an ocean. Sometimes they are powerful and knock us over; sometimes they simply lap at our feet. They are not good or bad; they are all a part of the vast ocean of our mind.

The feelings of being trapped or resentful will never just disappear. They may take on new story lines or circumstances, but they will always be a part of our lives, just like other feelings such as affection or jealousy. Whenever you find yourself in a claustrophobic situation with your feelings, you have a poignant choice. You can lean into them or run away from them.

Running away from your feelings is a bit like running from a heat-seeking missile. They will always find you; they have locked on to you and know exactly where you are going. In this case the only thing you are doing by running from them is exhausting yourself. The emotions will still catch up with you, only now you are even more drained and have to deal with them in this exhausted state.

However, if you lean into your feelings, you may find a form of liberation within them. If you are feeling trapped, the best way to get untrapped is to embrace whatever emotions arise for you, on or off the meditation cushion. If you are at work and you are spending eight hours a day lost in resentment, look at that resentment. Embrace it. Explore it, just as you explore a question or phrase during contemplation practice. You can see where it resides in your body or what shape or color it bears. The more you poke at the feeling of resentment, the less heavy it feels. This path of exploring resentment shows us how ephemeral this and other emotions truly are.

My friend and fellow Shambhala teacher Susan Piver has written, "A brilliant life is not about being untouched by sorrow but has more to do with relaxing and allowing the world to touch you."[8] Sorrow, resentment, pain—these emotions will touch us. There's no way around it. If you want to live a rich and full life, especially at work, you need to take those feelings on as part of your path. You have to see whatever obstacles arise as simply part of your meditation practice. Taking each challenge as an opportunity to let the world touch you is the Vajrayana path.

Another term for Vajrayana is *tantra*. *Tantra* can be translated in a number of ways, but the translation that has stuck in my mind over the years is "continuity." Tantra, in this regard, does not refer just to the vast plethora of practices, rituals, and teachings from the Buddhist tradition that analyzes reality. It points to the fact that in any moment we have the ability to wake up to our true selves, bursting through our emotional barriers as if they were paper. We can string together our moments of waking up to reality as it is. We can embody that continuity of awake even at a job in which we previously felt trapped.

The Vajrayana practices employ many skillful means of waking up that need to be offered to students by authorized teachers. However, we can all aspire to wake up on a moment-by-moment basis, seeing our resentment or other emotions not as challenges but as moments when we can come back to the present and see reality as it is. Through waking up to what is actually going on, as opposed to succumbing to the emotional storm that attempts to blur our vision, we are continuously waking up. Thus, your job that you feel trapped in, or that makes you feel resentment, is actually a perfectly good opportunity to practice meditation and become an authentic human being.

Part of being authentic is knowing when to hold 'em and when to fold 'em. The Buddha never said you should always grin and bear whatever horrible situation comes your way. If you have a mean boss or you feel unsuited for your position or you are constantly underappreciated, you can address those issues in a genuine and straightforward manner. Part of exploring and embracing tough emotional situations is making sure you can navigate through those storms in the kindest way possible, for yourself and for others. If your authentic truth is that you need to leave your place of employment, then you ought to follow through with that notion.

If you find that your resentment is more fleeting, then stay at your job and use it as an opportunity to continually come back to waking up, moment by moment, emotional trap by emotional trap. Your shitty job is an excellent training ground for enlightenment.

Always Trust Your Basic Goodness

I work in a really fast-paced, angry environment. It's often hard to keep up with what's going on—it all changes really quickly. When I try to slow things down within a group, it's considered an act of aggression. Is basic goodness even relevant in this sort of setting?

Basic goodness is always relevant. It is our birthright. It's that voice that whispers in your ear, after the longest, hardest day of your life, "It will get better." It's the part of you that falls in love, openly, wildly in love, even though you have been hurt before. It's the small aspect within you that knows that one more drink isn't a good idea or that taking on a new job or volunteer post would actually bring you a lot of happiness. It's gentle, discerning, kind, wise, and relevant to just this sort of situation.

When it comes to work, Sakyong Mipham Rinpoche has said, "What makes our life spiritual or worldly is not our vocation but our view."[9] You can view your place of employment as full of demon-like coworkers bent on making you miserable by prodding you with pitchforks made up of constantly changing rules, or you can relax and see it for what it is: work. If you can do three things—relax into the present moment, allow your *bodhicitta* to manifest, and have faith in your basic goodness— then your work will be your spiritual practice. All that it takes is this subtle shift in view.

The shift in view is to consider your workplace not as a hell realm, full of aggressive people, but as already sacred. It may not look the way you want it to, and people may not always behave the way you want them to, but it is in fact a sacred environment. You possess basic goodness, as does everyone else you work with. Even the biggest jerk at your office possesses basic goodness. Your mission, if you choose to accept it, is to help guide your coworkers to see that simple truth.

Let's break out those three things I mentioned above, which will help you perceive your work as sacred.

Be Present

We know that in any given moment we have the ability to cut through our habitual tendencies and come into the present moment. In a quick-paced meeting, a back-and-forth e-mail exchange, or a two-minute meeting over the telephone, we have the opportunity to pause and connect with what is. Maybe you are like the person who asked the question for this section and have tried to ask your colleagues to slow down, and maybe people have shot you a funny look when you did so.

There are times when things need to be done quickly and other times when you need to take your time. If you are fully present with each scenario, that arises you are most likely to read the situation and know which is which. From there you can suggest the most skillful means to address the situation and point out the logic around why you made such a suggestion. Even if your advice is to slow down, if you are reading the scenario clearly and have some basic logic around why that is important, people will tend to respect your words.

Allow Your Bodhicitta to Manifest

Never underestimate the power of an open heart. When someone is barking orders and running around like a chicken with its head cut off, a well-timed "How is your wife doing? I know she was sick recently" can transform the entire situation. Remember: *bodhicitta* isn't the weepy type of open-heartedness. *Bodhicitta* is tough. It is resilient. It is the powerhouse of compassion and getting beneficial acts done.

Last year I spent several months working on the Obama presidential reelection campaign. After we gave it our all and were burned to productive crisps, we woke up successful on November 7. I hadn't slept well in weeks and spent the majority of that day on the couch lounging with friends. Halfway through the day all staff throughout America was invited onto a conference call. The president wanted to thank us.

The five-minute speech he gave that day still brings tears to my eyes. It wasn't a policy speech or a traditional thank-you. It was about us. It was him saying how proud he was of us. Not just because we won the campaign but because he knew us and knew what we had done in the name of social justice, and he knew we would all go on to do great things. Just creating this cadre of devoted and brilliant leaders would have been reward enough for him; he had developed true faith in the future of our country through empowering his team.

As the president spoke, tears came to his eyes. As soon as he teared up, staff around the country met him in that open-hearted space and began to cry along with him. It was a moment of pure connection, whether you were in the room with him or listening on a couch in Ohio. We were all one in that moment.

I mention this story not to boast about what a genuine president we have (although we do) but to highlight that this man, our commander in chief, often leads our nation through letting his heart show. When the massacre in Newtown, Connecticut, occurred, he made a similarly moving speech and shared in the tears that were in the eyes of so many of us. If the leader of this nation can be brave enough to connect with people through the power of an open heart, we can too.

Have Faith in Your Basic Goodness

The more I practice meditation and study the teachings of Buddhism, the more I realize that it all comes down to this simple task: have confidence in your own ability to wake up. Have faith in your basic goodness. When you wake up in the morning, you have a choice: Do you want doubt to rule your life? Do you want to think you're not quick enough or smart enough or efficient enough to handle the quick-paced, aggressive work environment? Or do you want basic goodness to take the wheel and guide you through discernment and gentleness to act in whatever way is best in a given scenario?

The choice, in my opinion, is clear. You simply have to be brave enough to trust that you are basically good. Chögyam Trungpa Rinpoche once said, "Real warriors do not think in terms of challenge, nor are their minds occupied with the battlefield or with past or future consequences. The warrior is completely one with bravery, one with that particular moment."[10] In this moment we can connect to our basic goodness. If you are brave, do that. Do not think about the past and how things used to be. Do not fantasize about future consequences. Just be one with bravery and trust your basic goodness to guide you.

Through all of these topics, be it setting up a meditation practice, going out with friends, diving into your love life, finding a way to create positive social change, or even working in today's speedy, aggressive environment, basic goodness has something to offer you. If you have faith in your true nature, it will show you the way. In a well-known quote, Helen Keller said, "Life is either a daring adventure or nothing." Please have faith in yourself and make this life an adventure.

APPENDIX 1. SITTING MEDITATION INSTRUCTION

Shamatha, or calm-abiding meditation, is a practice that has existed for centuries. It is deceptive in its simplicity, as it may prove to be quite challenging to practice day-in and day-out. Try this practice out for ten minutes a day to start, and if you want to increase the amount of time per session after a few weeks, by all means do so.

Body

To begin, sit at the center of your cushion or chair. You want to feel balanced when you sit down to meditate. If you are sitting on a chair, place both feet firmly on the ground, about hip-width apart. If you are sitting on a cushion, sit cross-legged with your knees falling just a bit below your hips. Take a moment to feel the weight of your body on the earth.

From this strong base elongate your spine. If it helps, you can envision a string at the top of your head pulling you straight up, stretching your skeletal structure. Many of us are used to slouching, so this upright posture may initially feel uncomfortable. Stick with it. Relax the muscles in your shoulders and back. Try dropping your hands at your sides, then lift them up at the elbows and drop them palms down on your thighs.

This positioning should be a comfortable spot for your hands and also provide a bit of extra support for your back.

Allow your skull to rest atop your spine. Slightly tuck in your chin. Relax the muscles in your face, including those in your forehead, around your eyes, nose, and jaw. This may mean your jaw hangs open, which is encouraged. Place your tongue against the roof of your mouth, thus slowing down the swallowing process and allowing for clear breathing. Finally, rest your gaze two to four feet ahead of you on the ground in a loose and unfocused manner. This may sound odd, keeping your eyes open, but trust me on this one. If your intention is to wake up and be present for your everyday life, it makes sense to practice meditation with your eyes open.

You should feel grounded, dignified, and uplifted by your posture. This particular positioning allows you not to have to concentrate too much on "getting the posture right" or contorting yourself in an uncomfortable manner, but is relaxed enough that you can stay with the breath.

Breath

The breath is the object of your meditation. You do not need to do anything to it. You do not need to elongate your breaths or breathe in any particular way. Just let yourself breathe as you always do. The only difference here is that you are actually paying attention to it.

In particular, you bring your full attention to both the physical sensation of your out-breath and your in-breath.

Mind

After a few initial breaths you may notice that your mind drifts off into uncharted territory. You know that you want to stay with the breath but you catch yourself reliving a phone call that happened earlier that day or making big plans for your weekend. You are no longer in the here and now. You are lost in the past or future. When you catch yourself drifting off into fantasy, spinning out story lines around strong emotions, or flitting from one discursive thought to another, gently bring yourself back to the breath.

If it is helpful, you can silently say "thinking" to yourself as a reminder that your thoughts are not good or bad, but that what you really want to be doing is coming back to the breath. Whenever you get distracted, you can label your thoughts "thinking" and come back to your in-breath and your out-breath, anchoring yourself to the reality of this very moment. Please be gentle with yourself when you meditate.

APPENDIX 2. WALKING MEDITATION INSTRUCTION

We are always meditating on something. We might be meditating on how hungry we are or what we have to do later on in the day, but our mind is resting on something all the time. In walking meditation practice we are meditating on our physical movement. To begin, try this practice for seven minutes at a time, as often as you would like.

Begin by standing up. Ball your left hand up loosely and place it at your navel. Now place your right hand on top of it. Now walk. Slow it down, though. You can walk in a large circle or down a path in your neighborhood, but walk slower than you normally do.

Take the time to pay attention to your physical movement. Notice as you move your foot off the ground, as it soars through the air, you land on your heel, and then the rest of your foot descends as your other foot lifts off. Don't go so slow so that you're just taking one step at a time; walk fluidly like you always do, but slower and with more mindfulness.

Your gaze can be slightly below the horizon—best not to look at your feet. When you notice your mind has drifted off, as it does in shamatha meditation, use the same process of saying "thinking" to yourself, and come back to the physical sensation of your body moving through space.

NOTES

Introduction

1. Shunryu Suzuki Roshi, quoted in Pema Chödrön, *Practicing Peace in Times of War* (Boston: Shambhala Publications, 2006), p. 31.
2. Chögyam Trungpa, quoted in Pema Chödrön, *Living Beautifully* (Boston: Shambhala Publications, 2012).

Chapter 1. Wake Up Like a Buddha

1. Sakyong Mipham, *Ruling Your World* (New York: Three Rivers Press, 2006), p. 20.
2. Chögyam Trungpa, *Smile at Fear* (Boston: Shambhala Publications, 2009), p. 9.
3. Seung Sahn, *Only Don't Know* (Boston: Shambhala Publications, 1999), p. 3.
4. Dzongsar Jamyang Khyentse, *What Makes You Not a Buddhist* (Boston: Shambhala Publications, 2008), p. 87.
5. Sakyong Mipham, *Running with the Mind of Meditation* (New York: Harmony, 2012), p. 78.
6. Seung Sahn, *Only Don't Know*, p. 98.
7. Chögyam Trungpa, *Work, Sex, Money* (Boston: Shambhala Publications, 2011), p. 99.
8. Trungpa, *Smile at Fear*, p. 17.

9. Masajo Suzuki, from *Love Haiku*, trans. and ed. by Patricia Donegan (Boston: Shambhala Publications, 2009).
10. Chögyam Trungpa, *Training the Mind and Cultivating Loving-Kindness* (Boston: Shambhala Publications, 2003), p. 43.
11. Trungpa, *Smile at Fear*, p. 112.

Chapter 2. Play Like a Buddha

1. Pema Chödrön, *Living Beautifully* (Boston: Shambhala Publications, 2012), pp. 107–108.
2. Chögyam Trungpa, *The Myth of Freedom and the Way of Meditation* (Boston: Shambhala Publications, 2005), p. 56.
3. Dzongsar Khyentse, *What Makes You*, p. 67.
4. Chögyam Trungpa, *The Collected Works of Chögyam Trungpa*, vol. 8 (Boston: Shambhala Publications, 2004), p. 65.
5. Seung Sahn, *Only Don't Know*, pp. 14–15.
6. Ibid., p. 88.
7. Chödrön, *Living Beautifully*, p. 117.

Chapter 3. Getting It On Like a Buddha

1. Susan Piver, *The Wisdom of a Broken Heart* (New York: Free Press, 2010).
2. Trungpa, *Work, Sex, Money*, p. 119.
3. Ibid., p. 103.
4. Ibid.
5. Sakyong Mipham, *Ruling Your World*, p. 26.
6. Chödrön, *Living Beautifully*, p. 96.
7. Trungpa, *Work, Sex, Money*, p. 132.
8. Chödrön, *Living Beautifully*, p. 50.
9. Machik Labdrön, quoted in Pema Chödrön, *Start Where You Are* (Boston: Shambhala Publications, 2001), p. 49.
10. From *The Essential Chögyam Trungpa* (Boston: Shambhala Publications, 1999), p. 183.
11. Thich Nhat Hanh, *True Love* (Boston: Shambhala Publications, 2011), p. 1.

12. Sakyong Mipham, *Running with the Mind,* p. 111.
13. Sharon Salzberg, *Lovingkindness* (Boston: Shambhala Publications, 2002), p. 33.
14. Seung Sahn, *Only Don't Know,* p. 83.
15. Chögyam Trungpa, quoted in *Love Haiku* (Boston: Shambhala Publications, 2009), p. v.

Chapter 4. Change the World Like a Buddha

1. Sakyong Mipham, *The Shambhala Principle* (New York: Harmony Books, 2013), p. 43.
2. Chögyam Trungpa, *Shambhala: The Sacred Path of the Warrior* (Boston: Shambhala Publications, 2007), p. 29.
3. Samyutta Nikaya Sutra.
4. Seung Sahn, *Only Don't Know,* p. 3.
5. Salzberg, *Lovingkindness,* p. 16.
6. Chödrön, *Living Beautifully,* p. 67.
7. Ibid., p. 62.
8. Quoted in Sogyal, *The Tibetan Book of Living and Dying* (San Francisco: HarperSanFrancisco, 1994), p. 383.
9. Chödrön, *Living Beautifully,* p. 111.
10. Quoted in Sogyal, *Tibetan Book,* p. 383.
11. Pema Chödrön, *Taking the Leap* (Boston: Shambhala Publications, 2012), p. 27.
12. Shunryu Suzuki, *Zen Mind, Beginner's Mind* (Boston: Shambhala Publications, 2011), p. 32.
13. Michael Stone, *Awake in the World* (Boston: Shambhala Publications, 2011), p. 23.
14. Trungpa, *Smile at Fear,* p. 62.
15. Sakyong Mipham, *Shambhala Principle,* p. 167.
16. Khenpo Tsultrim Gyamtso Rinpoche, "Eight Orders for My Students," translated and put to melody by Ari Goldfield, Dec. 21, 1997; rev. February 6, 1998.
17. Trungpa, *Shambhala,* p. 26.
18. Chödrön, *Living Beautifully,* p. 107.

Chapter 5. Work Like a Buddha

1. Shantideva, *The Way of the Bodhisattva* (Padmakara translation) (Boston: Shambhala Publications, 2006), p. 73.
2. Sakyong Mipham, *Ruling Your World*, p. 177.
3. Ibid., p. 175.
4. Ibid., p. 176.
5. Michael Carroll, *Fearless at Work* (Boston: Shambhala Publications, 2012), p. 78.
6. Shantideva, *Way of the Bodhisattva*, p. 127.
7. Thich Nhat Hanh, *True Love*, p. 2.
8. Piver, *Wisdom*, p. 21.
9. Sakyong Mipham, *Ruling Your World*, p. 31.
10. Trungpa, *Smile at Fear*, p. 50.

RESOURCES

Further Reading

The Buddha Walks into a Bar by Lodro Rinzler. My first book.

Turning the Mind into an Ally by Sakyong Mipham Rinpoche. My recommended go-to read for the technique of meditation.

The Shambhala Principle by Sakyong Mipham Rinpoche. A beautiful manifesto on how to bring basic goodness into society.

Work, Sex, Money: Real Life on the Path of Mindfulness by Chögyam Trungpa Rinpoche. A lovely exposition on the intersection of everyday life and meditation.

Shambhala: The Sacred Path of the Warrior by Chögyam Trungpa Rinpoche. A foundational text on Shambhala Buddhism.

Ruling Your World by Sakyong Mipham Rinpoche. A great book overall, but a terrific exploration of the Six Ways of Ruling.

Only Don't Know by Zen Master Seung Sahn. Letters to and responses from a Zen master.

The 37 Practices of a Bodhisattva by Ngulchu Thogme. Each practice is worth spending at least a day contemplating.

Lovingkindness by Sharon Salzberg. Because the first step will always be offering love to yourself.

Comfortable with Uncertainty by Pema Chödrön. A compilation of teachings from Pema Chödrön, each chapter being short enough to read in a few minutes before bed.

Living Beautifully by Pema Chödrön. A terrific exposition on how to do just that.

The Wisdom of a Broken Heart by Susan Piver. An excellent read for anyone feeling heartbroken.

Awake at Work by Michael Carroll. Mr. Carroll has spent decades applying meditation principles to the workplace environment: a great read.

A Guide to the Bodhisattva's Way of Life (also known as *The Way of the Bodhisattva*) by Shantideva. A pivotal text on the Mahayana path.

One City: A Declaration of Interdependence by Ethan Nichtern. An exploration of interconnectivity.

Web Sites

www.lodrorinzler.com. My personal Web site with written, audio, and video teachings. There are also links to the work I do in the realm of authentic leadership training.

www.shambhala.org. Teachings and resources for supporting your meditation practice, including a list of Shambhala centers that you can visit for in-person teachings.

www.samadhicushions.com. A great source for meditation cushions, malas, and other supplies.

Contact Info

E-mail: info@lodrorinzler.com
Twitter: @lodrorinzler
Facebook: Lodro Rinzler
Bat Signal: A giant *L* will suffice.